1981

EUROPEAN ROMANTICISM

Self-Definition

EUROPEAN ROMANTICISM
Self-Definition

An anthology compiled by
Lilian R. Furst

METHUEN
London & New York

*First published in 1980 by Methuen & Co. Ltd
11 New Fetter Lane, London EC4P 4EE
Published in the USA by Methuen & Co.
in association with Methuen, Inc.
773 Third Avenue, New York, NY 10017
© 1980 Lilian R. Furst
Phototypeset in V.I.P. Plantin by
Western Printing Services Ltd, Bristol
Printed in the United States of America*

British Library Cataloguing in Publication Data

European romanticism.
  1. Romanticism – Addresses, essays, lectures
  *2. Literature, Modern – 19th century – History
  and criticism – Addresses, essays, lectures*
  I. Furst, Lilian Renee
  809'.914   PN751   79-40809

ISBN 0-416-71870-1
ISBN 0-416-71880-9 Pbk

I must Create a System or be enslav'd by another Man's.
I will not Reason & Compare: my business is to Create.

Blake, *Jerusalem*, *Complete Writings*, p. 629.

CONTENTS

II. ROMANTIC ART:
THE GUIDING PRINCIPLES

III. ROMANTIC ART: FORM AND GENRE

IV: DATA

PREFACE

The focus of this anthology is on self-definition. How did the Romantics envisage their own movement? In what terms did they formulate their aims and intentions? In delineating their poetics, which aspects and characteristics did they choose to emphasise? How did they conceive the various genres? In short, what did the Romantics themselves have to say about Romanticism?

The answers to such questions are fundamental to an understanding of what is meant and implied by European Romanticism. The long-range implications of Romanticism are perhaps even more important than its immediate effects and achievements, for in the poetic theory of the Romantics lie already the seeds of those aesthetic concepts on which much modern writing is based. Beneath the pressing concerns of the day, the attempts to define, explain and defend the new modes of perception and the new styles of expression, the Romantics were in fact confronting once again such central questions of aesthetics as the validity of good taste, the force of innovation as against traditionalism, the social function of art, the requisite of freedom for the artist. The ideas which they put forward from the closing years of the eighteenth century onwards were not only of striking originality at that time; they have also proven of lasting significance for subsequent thinking and writing. While the beauties of Romantic poetry have long been appreciated, the import of Romantic literary theory has still not been fully recognised.

In part at least this neglect may stem from the relative inaccessibility of most of the texts. A few, such as Wordsworth's *Preface to 'Lyrical Ballads'*, Shelley's *Defence of Poetry*, and Coleridge's *Biographia Literaria* present no difficulties, of course. However, these are rather the exceptions. Many of the major programmatic statements are either embedded in lengthy works or scattered in prefaces, fragments, and journals which are far from easy to locate. The purpose of this anthology is to bring together the basic theoretical pronouncements of the European Romantics so as to make the primary source material readily available in a single small volume. The intention is not to illustrate the chief characteristics of Romanticism, as has already been done in other anthologies, but to concentrate solely on that process of self-definition in which the Romantics engaged with such evident relish and which provides ultimately the surest key to comprehension.

As in any anthology, the problems of selection are inevitably formidable because of the richness of the field. Choices have to be made and limits set which may in some ways appear arbitrary. The temporal boundaries of this volume are 1797 to 1836, the apogee of the historical Romantic movement, though by no means its full extent in either direction. The literatures included – English, French, and German – represent the kernel of Romanticism. A wider geographic catchment, embracing Italy and Spain, was originally planned, but idealistic schemes are liable to modification in the face of the economic realities of pricing, and this was one such instance. The decision to exclude verse was less painful because most of the definitions are in prose anyway, and such poems as Coleridge's *Dejection: An Ode*, Wordsworth's *Tintern Abbey*, Keats' *Ode to Beauty*, and even the series of four *Nuits* by Musset are well-enough known to be found without difficulty.

The presentation is thematic. The first part covers concepts and general definitions. The second is devoted to the guiding principles of Romantic art, grouped under four major headings:

the function of art, the role of the artist, the creative imagination, and the shapes of beauty. These sub-sections arose organically out of the material itself in so far as these topics reflect the Romantics' major preoccupations. The final part is concerned with the actual forms and genres of Romantic art. There is in places some overlap from one section to another for certain passages deal with more than one facet of Romantic thought. But this is quite natural, and indeed serves to show that Romantic ideology is an essentially cohesive web of interlocking ideas, a *Weltanschauung*, a vision of the world in the literal sense of the term. Within the sections the extracts are arranged in chronological order. The chart (pp. 151–2) integrates all the works that have been cited; it also clearly illustrates the national historical pattern in the temporal sequence: a predominance of German works at the turn of the century, followed by a spate of English treatises, and then a burst of French manifestoes somewhat later. Each passage bears an exact reference to its source so that it can be replaced in its context by any reader wishing to follow it further. Wherever possible, the established text of a recent critical edition is used, whose typography (spelling, punctuation, italics, capitals) is reproduced. Brief biographical as well as bibliographical data are given at the end of the volume.

Every French and German passage is preceded by a translation. It has been my aim to keep these translations as close as was reasonable to the original and to avoid interpretative intrusions. A greater freedom would have allowed a smoother and more polished version, but this would have been at the expense of fidelity to the text, which seemed to me of paramount importance in an anthology designed to bring readers into direct contact with the primary sources. The juxtaposition of translation and foreign language text leads to a perhaps awkward reduplication. However, the translations are necessary because of the idiom that many of the Romantics favoured: inventive, imaginative, highly metaphorical, often complex or fragmentary in syntax, at times idiosyncratic in usage – frankly daunting to anyone not thoroughly familiar with the language (and on occasion even to those who are!). On the other hand, simply to offer translations would have defeated the main purpose of this anthology, the opportunity for an immediate confrontation of the tenets of Romanticism.

Indirectly this anthology also acts as a mirror to European Romanticism. The recurrent insistence on certain cardinal themes, such as the primacy of the creative imagination, the almost mystical function of art and the divine role of the poet, reveals a large measure of agreement on the fundamental beliefs which nurtured the Romantic movement. At the same time, points of dissension become evident too, and above all, differences of emphasis and of tone. The balance of interest in the genres, for instance, is sharply at variance. Drama is crucial to French Romanticism in its opposition to the Neoclassical tradition; yet it arouses little interest in Germany, and almost none in England where the Shakespearean theatre effectively preempted the need for such debate. Conversely, it is the English who gave the most searching consideration to the renewal of lyric poetry; the French, too, devoted much throught to this genre. By contrast, in Germany, where lyric poetry had already achieved a brilliant renaissance during the Storm and Stress movement of the 1770s, it attracts scant attention, whereas the narrative is subjected to closer scrutiny than elsewhere. The rhetoric and the approach display an even greater diversity, ranging from ecstatic rhapsodies to sober argument, from grandiose abstractions to concrete analyses, reflecting both the mode of the individual writer and the temper of his environment. In the mirror of its self-definition European Romanticism shows that intriguing multeity in unity that Coleridge identified as the essence of beauty.

I am indebted to the University of Texas at Dallas for a grant from organised research funds towards the cost of xeroxing and typing and for the services of a research assistant, C. Suzanne Grossman, whose willingness I much appreciated. I should also like to express my sincere gratitude to the librarians at the University of Texas at Austin and particularly at Southern Methodist University in Dallas for the courtesies always extended to me. Eileen Tollett had the superb ingenuity to find her way without fault through the maze of my first manuscript, which she typed with meticulous accuracy. Finally, my special thanks to two of my colleagues at Case Western Reserve University during my year's visit, Richard Barnett and Peter Salm, who tolerated my queries with such good humour, and who gave me expert advice on thorny points of translation.

Cleveland, Ohio   L.R.F.

PART I
CONCEPTS AND DEFINITIONS

THE WORLD MUST BE ROMANTICISED

NOVALIS

The world must be romanticised. So its original meaning will again be found. To romanticise is nothing other than an exponential heightening. In this process the lower self becomes identified with a better self. Just as we ourselves are part of such an exponential sequence. This process is still wholly unknown. By investing the commonplace with a lofty significance, the ordinary with a mysterious aspect, the familiar with the prestige of the unfamiliar, the finite with the semblance of infinity, thereby I romanticise it.

Die Welt muss romantisiert werden. So findet man den ursprünglichen Sinn wieder. Romantisieren ist nichts als eine qualitative Potenzierung. Das niedre Selbst wird mit einem bessern Selbst in dieser Operation identifiziert. So wie wir selbst eine solche qualitative Potenzreihe sind. Diese Operation ist noch ganz unbekannt. Indem ich dem Gemeinen einen hohen Sinn, dem Gewöhnlichen ein geheimnisvolles Ansehn, dem Bekannten die Würde des Unbekannten, dem Endlichen einen unendlichen Schein gebe, so romantisiere ich es.

(Fragmente des Jahres 1798, Gesammelte Werke, No. 879, vol. III, p. 38.)

*   *   *   *   *

The art to estrange in a pleasant manner, to make an object

seem strange yet familiar and attractive, that is romantic poetics.

Die Kunst, auf eine angenehme Art zu befremden, einen Gegenstand fremd zu machen und doch bekannt und anziehend, das ist die romantische Poetik.

(*Fragmente aus den letzten Jahren 1799–1800,*
Gesammelte Werke, No. 3053, vol. IV, p. 301.)

UNIVERSAL TRANSCENDENTAL POETRY

FRIEDRICH SCHLEGEL

Romantic poetry is a progressive universal poetry. It is destined not merely to reunite the separate genres of poetry and to link poetry to philosophy and rhetoric. It would and should also mingle and fuse poetry and prose, genius and criticism, artistic poetry and natural poetry, make poetry lively and sociable, and life and society poetic, poetise wit, fill and saturate the forms of art with worthy cultural matter of every kind, and animate them with a flow of humour. It embraces all that is poetic, from the greatest art system that enfolds further systems, down to the sigh, the kiss uttered in artless song by the child creating its own poetry. It can so identify with what is being represented that one might well think its sole aim was to characterise poetic individuals of every sort; but there is as yet no form designed fully to express the author's mind: so that some artists, who want only to write a novel, have come to portray themselves. Romantic poetry alone can, like the epic, become a mirror to the whole surrounding world, an image of its age. At the same time, free of all real and ideal interests, it can also float on wings of poetic reflection midway between the work and the artist, constantly reinforcing this reflection and multiplying it as in an unending series of mirrors. It has the potential for the highest, most manifold evolution by expanding not only outward but also inward, for each thing destined to be a whole entity is organised uniformly in all its parts, so that the prospect is opened up of a boundlessly developing classicism. Among the arts Romantic poetry is what wit is to philosophy, and what sociability, friendship and love are to life. Other types of poetry are complete and can now be wholly analysed. Romantic poetry is still in the process of becoming; this indeed is its very essence, that it is eternally evolving, never completed. It cannot be exhausted by any theory, and only a divinatory criticism could dare to try to characterise its ideal. It alone is infinite, just as it alone is free, recognising as its prime law that the poet's caprice brooks no law. Romantic poetry is the only type of poetry that is more than merely a type of poetry; it is in fact the very art of poetry itself: for in a certain sense all poetry is or should be romantic.

Die romantische Poesie ist eine progressive Universalpoesie. Ihre Bestimmung ist nicht bloss, alle getrennte Gattungen der Poesie wieder zu vereinigen, und die Poesie mit der Philosophie und Rhetorik in Berührung zu setzen. Sie will, und soll auch Poesie und Prosa, Genialität und Kritik, Kunstpoesie und Naturpoesie bald mischen, bald verschmelzen, die Poesie lebendig und gesellig, und das Leben und die Gesellschaft poetisch machen, den Witz poetisieren, und die Formen der Kunst mit gediegnem Bildungsstoff jeder Art anfüllen und sättigen, und durch die Schwingungen des Humors beseelen. Sie umfasst alles, was nur poetisch ist, vom grössten wieder mehrere Systeme in sich enthaltenden Systeme der Kunst, bis zu dem Seufzer, dem Kuss, den das dichtende Kind aushaucht in kunstlosen Gesang. Sie kann sich so in das Dargestellte verlieren, dass man glauben möchte, poetische Individuen jeder Art zu charakterisieren, sei ihr Eins und Alles; und doch gibt es noch keine Form, die so dazu gemacht wäre, den Geist des Autors vollständig auszudrücken: so dass manche Künstler, die nur auch einen Roman schreiben wollten, von ungefähr sich selbst dargestellt haben. Nur sie kann gleich dem Epos ein

Spiegel der ganzen umgebenden Welt, ein Bild des Zeitalters werden. Und doch kann auch sie am meisten zwischen dem Dargestellten und dem Darstellenden, frei von allem realen und idealen Interesse auf den Flügeln der poetischen Reflexion in der Mitte schweben, diese Reflexion immer wieder potenzieren und wie in einer endlosen Reihe von Spiegeln vervielfachen. Sie ist der höchsten und der allseitigsten Bildung fähig; nicht bloss von innen heraus, sondern auch von aussen hinein; indem sie jedem, was ein Ganzes in ihren Produkten sein soll, alle Teile ähnlich organisiert, wodurch ihr die Aussicht auf eine grenzenlos wachsende Klassizität eröffnet wird. Die romantische Poesie ist unter den Künsten was der Witz der Philosophie, und die Gesellschaft, Umgang, Freundschaft und Liebe im Leben ist. Andre Dichtarten sind fertig, und können nun vollständig zergliedert werden. Die romantische Dichtart ist noch im Werden; ja das ist ihr eigentliches Wesen, dass sie ewig nur werden, nie vollendet sein kann. Sie kann durch keine Theorie erschöpft werden, und nur eine divinatorische Kritik dürfte es wagen, ihr Ideal charakterisieren zu wollen. Sie allein ist unendlich, wie sie allein frei ist, und das als ihr erstes Gesetz anerkennt, dass die Willkür des Dichters kein Gesetz über sich leide. Die romantische Dichtart ist die einzige, die mehr als Art, und gleichsam die Dichtkunst selbst ist: denn in einem gewissen Sinn ist oder soll alle Poesie romantisch sein.

(*Athenäum Fragment*, No. 116, *Kritische Ausgabe*, vol. II, pp. 182–3.)

*   *   *   *   *

There is a type of poetry whose alpha and omega is the relationship of the ideal and the real, and which must, on the analogy of philosophical terminology, be called transcendental poetry. It begins as satire with the absolute distinction between ideal and real, is poised between the two in elegy, and finally achieves complete identity of the two in the idyll. But just as one

would attach little importance to a transcendental philosophy
that was not critical, that did not represent the act of producing
as well as the product, and did not also contain within its system
of transcendental thoughts a characterisation of transcendental
thinking: the same also holds true of this poetry which unites, in
modern poets, transcendental notions and ideas for a poetic
theory of the creative act with artistic contemplation and self-
portrayal, such as is found in Pindar, in Greek lyrical fragments
and ancient elegies, and more recently in Goethe; in each of its
representations it should also represent itself, and always be at
one and the same time poetry and poetry of poetry.

Es gibt eine Poesie, deren eins und alles das Verhältnis des
Idealen und des Realen ist, und die also nach der Analogie der
philosophischen Kunstsprache Transzendentalpoesie heissen
müsste. Sie beginnt als Satire mit der absoluten Ver-
schiedenheit des Idealen und Realen, schwebt als Elegie in der
Mitte, und endigt als Idylle mit der absoluten Identität beider.
So wie man aber wenig Wert auf eine Transzendental-
philosophie legen würde, die nicht kritisch wäre, nicht auch das
Produzierende mit dem Produkt darstellte, und im System der
transzendentalen Gedanken zugleich eine Charakteristik des
transzendentalen Denkens enthielte: so sollte wohl auch jene
Poesie die in modernen Dichtern nicht seltnen transzendentalen
Materialien und Vorübungen zu einer poetischen Theorie des
Dichtungsvermögens mit der künstlerischen Reflexion und
schönen Selbstbespiegelung, die sich im Pindar, den lyrischen
Fragmenten der Griechen, und der alten Elegie, unter den
Neuern aber in Goethe findet, vereinigen, und in jeder ihrer
Darstellungen sich selbst mit darstellen, und überall zugleich
Poesie und Poesie der Poesie sein.

(*Athenäum Fragment*, No. 238, *Kritische Ausgabe*,
vol. II, p. 204.)

*   *   *   *   *

For in my view and according to my usage, that is romantic that portrays emotional matter in an imaginative form. . . .

[. . .]

What then is meant by the Emotional? That which appeals to us, wherein feeling is predominant, not a sensual but a spiritual feeling. The source and soul of all these impulses resides in love, and the spirit of love must permeate romantic poetry, everywhere present in an invisibly visible manner; this is the intent of the above definition.

Denn nach meiner Ansicht und nach meinem Sprachgebrauch ist eben das romantisch, was uns einen sentimentalen Stoff in einer fantastischen Form darstellt. . . .

[. . .]

Was ist denn nun dieses Sentimentale? Das was uns anspricht, wo das Gefühl herrscht, und zwar nicht ein sinnliches, sondern das geistige. Die Quelle und Seele aller dieser Regungen ist die Liebe, und der Geist der Liebe muss in der romantischen Poesie überall unsichtbar sichtbar schweben; das soll jene Definition sagen.

(*Gespräch über die Poesie*, *Kritische Ausgabe*, vol. II, p. 333.)

*   *   *   *   *

I have identified a specific trait of the contrast between the Ancient and the Romantic. However, I beg you not to jump to the conclusion, that the Romantic and the Modern are synonymous for me. I think they are just as different as the paintings of Raphael and Correggio are from the etchings in fashion nowadays. If you want to clarify the difference, please read *Emilia Galotti*, which is so extremely modern yet not in the least romantic, and cast your mind back to Shakespeare, in whom I should like to posit the true centre, the kernel of romantic imagination. I seek and find the Romantic among the older Moderns, in Shakespeare, in Cervantes, in Italian poetry, in that age of chivalry, love and fable, from which the phenomenon and the word itself are derived.

[. . .]

But mark well this distinction, that the Romantic is not only a type of poetry but also an element of all poetry, that may be more or less in the forefront or in the background, but that must never be wholly absent. It must be obvious to you from my views, that and why I demand that all poetry should be romantic.

Ich habe ein bestimmtes Merkmal des Gegensatzes zwischen dem Antiken und dem Romantischen aufgestellt. Indessen bitte ich Sie doch, nun nicht sogleich anzunehmen, dass mir das Romantische und das Moderne völlig gleich gelte. Ich denke es ist etwa ebenso verschieden, wie die Gemälde des Raffael und Correggio von den Kupferstichen die jetzt Mode sind. Wollen Sie sich den Unterschied völlig klar machen, so lesen Sie gefälligst etwa die *Emilia Galotti* die so unaussprechlich modern und doch im geringsten nicht romantisch ist, und erinnern sich dann an Shakespeare, in den ich das eigentliche Zentrum, den Kern der romantischen Fantasie setzen möchte. Da suche und finde ich das Romantische, bei den ältern Modernen, bei Shakespeare, Cervantes, in der italiänischen Poesie, in jenem Zeitalter der Ritter, der Liebe und der Märchen, aus welchem die Sache und das Wort selbst herstammt.

[. . .]

Nur mit dem Unterschiede, dass das Romantische nicht sowohl eine Gattung ist als ein Element der Poesie, das mehr oder minder herrschen und zurücktreten, aber nie ganz fehlen darf. Es muss Ihnen nach meiner Ansicht einleuchtend sein, dass und warum ich fordre, alle Poesie solle romantisch sein.

(*Gespräch über die Poesie, Kritische Ausgabe*, vol. II, p. 335.)

SPONTANEOUS OVERFLOW OF POWERFUL FEELINGS

WILLIAM WORDSWORTH

Several of my Friends are anxious for the success of these Poems, from a belief that, if the views with which they were composed were indeed realised, a class of Poetry would be produced, well adapted to interest mankind permanently, and not unimportant in the quality and in the multiplicity of its moral relations: and on this account they have advised me to prefix a systematic defence of the theory upon which the Poems were written. But I was unwilling to undertake the task, knowing that on this occasion the Reader would look coldly upon my arguments, since I might be suspected of having been principally influenced by the selfish and foolish hope of *reasoning* him into an approbation of these particular Poems: and I was still more unwilling to undertake the task, because adequately to display the opinions, and fully to enforce the arguments, would require a space wholly disproportionate to a preface. For, to treat the subject with the clearness and coherence of which it is susceptible, it would be necessary to give a full account of the present state of the public taste in this country, and to determine how far this taste is healthy or depraved; which, again, could not be determined without pointing out in what manner language and the human mind act and re-act on each other, and without retracing the revolutions, not of literature alone, but likewise of society itself. I have therefore altogether declined to enter regularly upon this defence; yet I am sensible that there would be something like impropriety in abruptly obtruding upon the Public, without a few words of introduction, Poems so materially different from those upon which general approbation is at present bestowed.

It is supposed that by the act of writing in verse an Author makes a formal engagement that he will gratify certain known habits of association; that he not only thus apprises the Reader that certain classes of ideas and expressions will be found in his book, but that others will be carefully excluded. This exponent or symbol held forth by metrical language must in different areas of literature have excited very different expectations: for example, in the age of Catullus, Terence, and Lucretius, and that of Statius or Claudian; and in our own country, in the age of Shakespeare and Beaumont and Fletcher, and that of Donne and Cowley, or Dryden, or Pope. I will not take upon me to determine the exact import of the promise which, by the act of writing in verse, an Author in the present day makes to his reader; but it will undoubtedly appear to many persons that I have not fulfilled the terms of an engagement thus voluntarily contracted. They who have been accustomed to the gaudiness and inane phraseology of many modern writers, if they persist in reading this book to its conclusion, will, no doubt, frequently have to struggle with feelings of strangeness and awkwardness: they will look round for poetry, and will be induced to inquire by what species of courtesy these attempts can be permitted to assume that title. I hope, therefore, the reader will not censure me for attempting to state what I have proposed to myself to perform; and also (as far as the limits of a preface will permit) to explain some of the chief reasons which have determined me in the choice of my purpose: that at least he may be spared any unpleasant feeling of disappointment, and that I myself may be protected from one of the most dishonourable accusations which can be brought against an Author; namely, that of an indolence which prevents him from endeavouring to ascertain what is his duty, or, when his duty is ascertained, prevents him from performing it.

The principal object, then, proposed in these Poems, was to choose incidents and situations from common life, and to relate or describe them throughout, as far as was possible, in a selection of language really used by men, and, at the same time, to throw over them a certain colouring of imagination, whereby ordinary things should be presented to the mind in an unusual aspect; and further, and above all, to make these incidents and situations interesting by tracing in them, truly though not ostentatiously, the primary laws of our nature: chiefly, as far as regards the manner in which we associate ideas in a state of excitement. Humble and rustic life was generally chosen, because in that condition the essential passions of the heart find a better soil in which they can attain their maturity, are less under restraint, and speak a plainer and more emphatic language; because in that condition of life our elementary feelings coexist in a state of greater simplicity, and, consequently, may be more accurately contemplated, and more forcibly communicated; because the manners of rural life germinate from those elementary feelings, and, from the necessary character of rural occupations, are more easily comprehended, and are more durable; and, lastly, because in that condition the passions of men are incorporated with the beautiful and permanent forms of nature. The language, too, of these men has been adopted (purified indeed from what appear to be its real defects, from all lasting and rational causes of dislike or disgust), because such men hourly communicate with the best objects from which the best part of language is originally derived; and because, from their rank in society and the sameness and narrow circle of their intercourse, being less under the influence of social vanity, they convey their feelings and notions in simple and unelaborated expressions. Accordingly, such a language, arising out of repeated experience and regular feelings, is a more permanent, and a far more philosophical language, than that which is frequently substituted for it by Poets, who think that they are conferring honour upon themselves and their art in proportion as they separate themselves from the sympathies of men, and indulge in arbitrary and capricious habits of expression, in order to furnish food for fickle tastes and fickle appetites of their own creation.

I cannot, however, be insensible to the present outcry against the triviality and meanness, both of thought and language, which some of my contemporaries have occasionally introduced into their metrical compositions; and I acknowledge that this defect, where it exists, is more dishonourable to the Writer's own character than false refinement or arbitrary innovation, though I should contend at the same time that it is far less pernicious in the sum of its consequences. From such verses the Poems in these volumes will be found distinguished at least by one mark of difference, that each of them has a worthy *purpose*. Not that I always began to write with a distinct purpose formally conceived, but habits of meditation have, I trust, so prompted and regulated my feelings, that my descriptions of such objects as strongly excite those feelings will be found to carry along with them a *purpose*. If this opinion be erroneous, I can have little right to the name of a Poet. For all good poetry is the spontaneous overflow of powerful feelings: and though this be true, Poems to which any value can be attached were never produced on any variety of subjects but by a man who, being possessed of more than usual organic sensibility, had also thought long and deeply. For our continued influxes of feeling are modified and directed by our thoughts, which are indeed the representatives of all our past feelings; and as, by contemplating the relation of these general representatives to each other, we discover what is really important to men, so, by the repetition and continuance of this act, our feelings will be connected with important subjects, till at length, if we be originally possessed of much sensibility, such habits of mind will be produced that, by obeying blindly and mechanically the impulses of those habits, we shall describe objects, and utter sentiments, of such a nature, and in such connection with each other, that the understanding of the Reader must necessarily be in some degree enlightened, and his affection strengthened and purified.

(*Preface to 'Lyrical Ballads'*, *Poetical Works*, vol. II, pp. 385–8.)

THE LITERATURE OF THE NORTH

MME. DE STAËL

There are, I think, two quite distinct literatures, one from the South and the other from the North, with Homer as the prime source for the former, and Ossian for the latter. The Greeks, the Romans, the Italians, the Spanish, and the French of the age of Louis XIV adhere to the type of literature I shall call the literature of the South. English and German works, and some by Danes and Swedes must be classified as literature of the North, which began with the Scottish bards, the Icelandic fables and the Scandinavian poets. Before characterising the English and German writers, we have to consider in general the principal differences between the two literary hemispheres.

The English and Germans have undoubtedly often imitated the Ancients. They have learned some useful lessons from that fruitful study; but the original beauties of their works, bearing the imprint of Northern mythology, have a certain family likeness, a certain poetic grandeur, for which Ossian is the ultimate model. The English poets, it might be said, are outstanding for their philosophical spirit, which is evident in all their works; but Ossian hardly ever has any reflections: he simply narrates a sequence of events and impressions. My response to that objection is that the images and thoughts most common in Ossian are those that evoke the transience of life, veneration for the dead, glorification of their memory, adoration of those who have gone by those still here. If the poet has not added to these feelings any moral maxims or philosophical reflections, it is because at that time the human mind was not yet capable of the abstraction required to draw such conclusions. But the Ossianic songs stir the imagination in such a way as to stimulate profound meditation.

Melancholy poetry is that most in tune with philosophy. Sadness goes deeper into man's character and destiny than any other mood. The English poets, successors of the Scottish bards, incorporated into their representations the reflections and ideas inspired by them; but they kept the Northern imagination that delights in the seashore, the sound of the wind, the wild heaths; the imagination that carries the weary soul into the future and into another world. The imagination of Northern men soars beyond this earth, on which they live; it soars through the clouds on the horizon that are like the mysterious gateway from life into eternity.

One cannot make an outright choice between the two kinds of poetry, of which Homer and Ossian are the primary models. All my impressions, all my ideas make me incline toward the literature of the North; but my aim now is to analyse its distinctive features.

Climate is certainly one of the main reasons for the differences between the images that find favour in the North and those that are recalled with pleasure in the South.

[. .]

The poetry of the North is much more suited than that of the South to the mentality of a free nation. The first known originators of the literature of the South, the Athenians, were the nation most eager for independence. Nevertheless, it was easier to press the Greeks into servitude than Northerners. Love of the arts, the beauty of the climate, all the pleasures offered to the Athenians could serve as a compensation. Independence was the first and sole happiness of the Northern nations. A certain pride, a superiority to life, engendered by both the harshness of the earth and the gloom of the sky, made servitude intolerable; and long before the theory of constitutions and the advantages of representative government were known in England, the warlike spirit, celebrated with such enthusiasm in the Gaelic and Scandinavian poems, gave man a lofty notion of his individual strength and willpower. Independence existed for each person before liberty was established for all.

During the literary renewal, philosophy began with the

Northern nations, whose religious customs contained far less prejudices for reason to oppose than those of the Southern nations. The old poetry of the North presupposes much less superstition than does Greek mythology.

[.   .]

I have no intention of comparing the genius of Homer with that of Ossian. What we know of Ossian can hardly be considered a work; it is a collection of popular songs that used to be recited in the mountains of Scotland. Long-standing traditions no doubt existed in Greece before Homer composed his poem. Ossian's poems are no further in poetic art than Greek songs before Homer. So there is no real parity between the Iliad and Fingal's Song. Still, one can assess whether the images of nature, as they are represented in the South, arouse emotions as pure and noble as those in the North; whether the images of the South, in some respects more brilliant, stimulate as many thoughts and are as intimately linked to the soul's responses. Philosophical ideas associate, as if spontaneously, with sombre images. The poetry of the South, far from harmonising with meditation, like that of the North, and inspiring, as it were, what reflection must prove – this voluptuous poetry almost excludes ideas of a certain kind.

[.   .]

Finally, what gives the modern nations of the North a more philosophical turn of mind on the whole than the Southerners is the Protestant religion adopted by nearly all these nations. The Reformation is the historical period that most effectively fostered the perfectibility of the human race.

[.   .]

In France, the literature of the North is criticised for lacking taste. The writers of the North reply that taste is a purely arbitrary law that often deprives feeling and thought of their most original beauties. A compromise is, I think, possible between these two opinions. The rules of taste are not by any means arbitrary; the basic principles, in which universal truths are founded, must not be confused with the modifications arising out of local conditions.

[. . .]

The question is often put: Must genius be sacrificed to taste? No, certainly not; taste never requires the sacrifice of genius. In the literature of the North you often find ridiculous scenes alongside great beauties; and what should have been cut is what taste condemns. There is no inevitable connection between defects and beauties other than human weakness, which cannot go on sustaining the same loftiness. The defects are in no way consequential to the beauties; they can make us oblivious of the defects. But far from adding any lustre to a talented writer, often the defects weaken the impression he should make.

If one asks, which is preferable: a work with great defects and great beauties, or a mediocre but correct work, I shall answer without hesitation in favour of the former, where there is even only a single trait of genius.

[. . .]

Among Northern men of letters there is a peculiarity, determined, so to speak, more by partisanship than by judgement. They are almost so attached to their writers' defects as to their beauties; whereas they should say, like a clever woman speaking of a hero's weakness: *It is in spite of that, and not because of that, that he is great*.

It is pleasing impressions that are sought in masterpieces of the imagination. Now, taste is merely the art of knowing and foreseeing what can elicit these impressions. When you evoke repulsive objects, you arouse an unpleasant impression that would be deliberately avoided in reality; when you change moral terror into physical fright through the representation of scenes horrible in themselves, you forfeit all the attractiveness of the portrayal, you only give the nerves a shock, and you may fail to achieve even this painful effect, if you have tried to carry it too far; for in the theatre, as in life, once the exaggeration is grasped, even the true is no longer taken seriously. If you drag out the plot, if you make the speeches obscure and the events improbable, you lose or dissipate the audience's interest by overtaxing its attention. If you juxtapose base scenes with heroic characters, there is a danger that you will have difficulty in reestablishing the theatrical illusion; for it is extremely delicate in nature; and the slightest disturbance can break the spell for the spectators. The simple is restful to the mind, and renews its strength; but the common could even preclude the possibility of a return to noble and lofty thoughts.

In England, the beauties of Shakespeare can outweigh his defects; but they greatly diminish his reputation among other nations. Surprise is certainly an excellent means for heightening dramatic effect; but it would be absurd to draw the conclusion that a tragic scene should be preceded by a comic one in order to increase our surprise through the contrast. A beautiful feature in the midst of crass carelessness can be the more striking; but on the whole, the loss is greater than the gain. Surprise should stem from loftiness in itself, and not from the antithesis to pettiness of any kind. Painting needs shadows, but not blemishes, to bring out the brilliance of the colours. Literature ought to follow the same principles. Nature offers the model, and good taste should only be the considered observation of nature.

These ideas could be developed much further; but this suffices to prove that in literature taste never demands the sacrifice of any enjoyment; it points, on the contrary, to the means of increasing pleasure; and far from principles of taste being incompatible with genius, it is through the study of genius that those principles have been discovered.

I shall certainly not reproach Shakespeare for having departed from the rules of art; they are infinitely less important than those of taste, because these prescribe what should be done, while the former merely prohibit what should be avoided. There can be no mistaking what is bad, whereas it is impossible to set any limitations on the varied inventions of a man of genius; he can explore entirely new paths without, however, missing his goal. The rules of art calculate the probabilities for success; and if one succeeds, it matters little whether one has submitted to these rules, or not. But it is quite different in regard to taste; for to set oneself above it is a deviation from the very beauty of nature itself, and nothing can be above that.

Let us not say, therefore, that Shakespeare knew how to dispense with taste and to be superior to its laws. Let us recognise, on the contrary, that he has taste when he is sublime, and that he lacks taste whenever his talent falters.

Il existe, ce me semble, deux littératures tout-à-fait distinctes, celle qui vient du midi et celle qui descend du nord, celle dont Homère est la première source, celle dont Ossian est l'origine. Les Grecs, les Latins, les Italiens, les Espagnols, et les Français du siècle de Louis XIV, appartiennent au genre de littérature que j'appellerai la littérature du midi. Les ouvrages anglais, les ouvrages allemands, et quelques écrits des Danois et des Suédois, doivent être classés dans la littérature du nord, dans celle qui a commencé par les Bardes Ecossais, les Fables Islandaises, et les Poésies Scandinaves. Avant de caractériser les écrivains anglais et les écrivains allemands, il me paroît nécessaire de considérer d'une manière générale les principales différences des deux hémisphères de la littérature.

Les Anglais et les Allemands ont, sans doute, souvent imité les anciens. Ils ont retiré d'utiles leçons de cette étude féconde; mais leurs beautés originales portant l'empreinte de la mythologie du nord, ont une sorte de ressemblance, une certaine grandeur poétique dont Ossian est le premier type. Les poètes anglais, pourra-t-on dire, sont remarquables par leur esprit philosophique; il se peint dans tous leurs ouvrages; mais Ossian n'a presque jamais d'idées réfléchies: il raconte une suite d'événemens et d'impressions. Je réponds à cette objection que les images et les pensées les plus habituelles, dans Ossian, sont celles qui rappellent la brièveté de la vie, le respect pour les morts, l'illustration de leur mémoire, le culte de ceux qui restent envers ceux qui ne sont plus. Si le poète n'a point réuni à ces sentiments des maximes de morale ni des réflexions philosophiques, c'est qu'à cette époque l'esprit humain n'étoit point encore susceptible de l'abstraction nécessaire pour concevoir beaucoup de résultats. Mais l'ébranlement que les chants ossianiques causent à l'imagination, dispose la pensée aux méditations les plus profondes.

La poésie mélancolique est la poésie la plus d'accord avec la philosophie. La tristesse fait pénétrer bien plus avant dans le caractère et la destinée de l'homme, que toute autre disposition de l'âme. Les poètes anglais qui ont succédé aux Bards Ecossais, ont ajouté à leurs tableaux les réflexions et les idées que ces tableaux même devoient faire naître; mais ils ont conservé l'imagination du nord, celle qui se plaît sur le bord de la mer, au bruit des vents, dans les bruyères sauvages; celle enfin qui porte vers l'avenir, vers un autre monde, l'âme fatiguée de sa destinée. L'imagination des hommes du nord s'élance au delà de cette terre dont ils habitoient les confins; elle s'élance à travers les nuages qui bordent leur horizon, et semblent représenter l'obscur passage de la vie à l'éternité.

L'on ne peut décider d'une manière générale entre les deux genres de poésie dont Homère et Ossian sont comme les premiers modèles. Toutes mes impressions, toutes mes idées me portent de préférence vers la littérature du nord; mais ce dont il s'agit maintenant, c'est d'examiner ses caractères distinctifs.

Le climat est certainement l'une des raisons principales des différences qui existent entre les images qui plaisent dans le nord, et celles qu'on aime à se rappeler dans le midi.

[. . .]

La poésie du nord convient beaucoup plus que celle du midi à l'esprit d'un peuple libre. Les premiers inventeurs connus de la littérature du midi, les Athéniens, ont été la nation du monde la plus jalouse de son indépendance. Néanmoins il étoit plus facile de façonner à la servitude les Grecs que les hommes du nord. L'amour des arts, la beauté du climat, toutes ces jouissances prodiguées aux Athéniens, pouvoient leur servir de dédommagement. L'indépendance étoit le premier et l'unique bonheur des peuples septentrionaux. Une certaine fierté d'âme, un détachement de la vie, que font naître, et l'âpreté du sol, et la tristesse du ciel, devoient rendre la servitude insupportable; et long-temps avant que l'on connût en Angleterre, et la théorie des constitutions, et l'avantage des gouvernemens représentatifs, l'esprit guerrier que les poésies Erses et Scandinaves chantent avec tant d'enthousiasme, donnoit à l'homme une idée prodigieuse de sa force individuelle et de la puissance de sa volonté. L'indépendance existoit pour chacun, avant que la liberté fut constituée pour tous.

La philosophie, à la renaissance des lettres, a commencé par les nations septentrionales, dans les habitudes religieuses desquels la raison trouvoit à combattre infiniment moins de préjugés que dans celles des peuples méridionaux. La poésie antique du nord suppose beaucoup moins de superstition que la mythologie grecque.

[. . .]

Je suis loin de comparer le génie d'Homère à celui d'Ossian. Ce que nous connoissons d'Ossian ne peut être considéré comme un ouvrage; c'est un recueil des chansons populaires qui se répétoient dans les montagnes d'Ecosse. Avant qu'Homère eût composé son poëme, d'anciennes traditions existoient sans doute en Grèce. Les poésies d'Ossian ne sont pas plus avancées dans l'art poétique, que ne devoient l'être les chants des Grecs avant Homère. Aucune parité ne peut donc être établie avec justice entre l'Iliade et le poëme de Fingal. Mais on peut toujours juger si les images de la nature, telles qu'elles sont représentées dans le midi, excitent des émotions aussi nobles et aussi pures que celles du nord; si les images du midi, plus brillantes à quelques égards, font naître autant de pensées, ont un rapport aussi immédiat avec les sentimens de l'âme. Les idées philosophiques s'unissent comme d'elles-mêmes aux images sombres. La poésie du midi, loin de s'accorder, comme celle du nord, avec la méditation, et d'inspirer, pour ainsi dire, ce que la réflexion doit prouver; la poésie voluptueuse exclut presqu'entièrement les idées d'un certain ordre.

[. . .]

Enfin ce qui donne en général aux peuples modernes du nord un esprit plus philosophique qu'aux habitans du midi, c'est la religion protestante que ces peuples ont presque tous adoptée. La réformation est l'époque de l'histoire qui a le plus efficacement servi la perfectibilité de l'espèce humaine.

[. . .]

On reproche, en France, à la littérature du nord de manquer de goût. Les écrivains du nord répondent que ce goût est une législation purement arbitraire, qui prive souvent le sentiment et la pensée de leurs beautés les plus originales. Il existe, je crois, un point juste entre ces deux opinions. Les règles du goût ne sont point arbitraires; il ne faut pas confondre les bases principales sur lesquelles les vérités universelles sont fondées avec les modifications causées par les circonstances locales.

[. . .]

On dit souvent: Faut-il sacrifier le génie au goût? Non, sans doute; mais jamais le goût n'exige le sacrifice du génie. Vous trouvez souvent dans la littérature du nord des scènes ridicules à coté de grandes beautés. Ce qui est de bon goût dans de tels écrits, ce sont les grandes beautés; et ce qu'il falloit en retrancher, c'est ce que le goût condamne. Il n'existe de connexion nécessaire entre les défauts et les beautés, que par la foiblesse humaine, qui ne permet pas de se soutenir toujours à la même hauteur. Les défauts ne sont point une conséquence des beautés; elles peuvent les faire oublier. Mais loin que ces défauts prêtent au talent aucun éclat, souvent ils affoiblissent l'impression qu'il doit produire.

Si l'on demande ce qui vaut mieux d'un ouvrage avec de grands défauts et de grandes beautés, ou d'un ouvrage médiocre et correct, je répondrai, sans hésiter, qu'il faut préférer l'ouvrage où il existe, ne fût-ce qu'un seul trait de génie.

[. . .]

Parmi les hommes de lettres du nord, il existe une bizarrerie qui dépend plus, pour ainsi dire, de l'esprit de parti que du jugement. Ils tiennent aux défauts de leurs écrivains presqu'autant qu'à leurs beautés; tandis qu'ils devroient se dire, comme une femme d'esprit, en parlant des foiblesses d'un héros: *C'est malgré cela, et non à cause de cela, qu'il est grand.*

Ce que l'homme cherche dans les chefs-d'œuvre de l'imagination, ce sont des impressions agréables. Or le goût n'est que l'art de connoître et de prévoir ce qui peut causer ces impressions. Quand vous rappelez des objets dégoûtans, vous excitez une impression fâcheuse, qu'on fuiroit avec soin dans la réalité; quand vous changez la terreur morale en effroi physique, par la représentation de scènes horribles en elles-mêmes, vous perdez tout le charme de l'imitation, vous ne donnez qu'une commotion nerveuse, et vous pouvez manquer jusqu'à ce pénible effet, si vous avez voulu le pousser trop loin: car au théâtre, comme dans la vie, quand l'exagération est apperçue, on ne tient plus compte, même du vrai. Si vous prolongez les développemens, si vous mettez de l'obscurité dans les discours ou de l'invraisemblance dans les événemens, vous suspendez ou vous détruisez l'intérêt par la fatigue de l'attention. Si vous rapprochez des tableaux ignobles de personnages héroïques, il est à craindre qu'il vous soit difficile de faire renaître l'illusion théâtrale: elle est d'une nature extrêmement délicate; et la plus légère circonstance peut tirer les spectateurs de leur echantement. Ce qui est simple repose la pensée, et lui donne de nouvelles forces; mais ce qui est bas pourroit ôter jusqu'à la possibilité de reprendre à l'intérêt des pensées nobles et relevées.

Les beautés de Shakespear peuvent, en Angleterre triompher

de ses défauts: mais ils diminuent beaucoup de sa gloire parmi les autres nations. La surprise est certainement un grand moyen d'ajouter à l'effet; mais il seroit ridicule d'en conclure que l'on doive faire précéder une scène tragique d'une scène comique, pour augmenter l'étonnement par le contraste. Un beau trait, au milieu de négligences grossières, peut frapper davantage l'esprit; mais l'ensemble y perd plus que ne peut y gagner l'exception. La surprise doit naître de la grandeur en elle-même, et non de son opposition avec les petitesses, de quelque genre qu'elles soient. La peinture veut des ombres, mais non pas des taches pour relever l'éclat des couleurs. La littérature doit suivre les mêmes principes. La nature en offre le modèle, et le bon goût ne doit être que l'observation raisonnée de la nature.

On pourroit pousser beaucoup plus loin ces développemens; mais il suffit de prouver que le goût, en littérature, n'exige jamais le sacrifice d'aucune jouissance: il indique, au contraire, les moyens de les augmenter; et loin que les principes du goût soient incompatibles avec le génie, c'est en étudiant le génie qu'on a découvert ces principes.

Je ne reprocherai point à Shakespear de s'être affranchi des règles de l'art; elles ont infiniment moins d'importance que celles du goût, parce que les unes prescrivent ce qu'il faut faire, et que les autres se bornent à défendre ce qu'on doit éviter. L'on ne peut se tromper sur ce qui est mauvais, tandis qu'il est impossible de tracer des limites aux diverses combinaisons d'un homme de génie; il peut suivre des routes entièrement nouvelles, sans manquer cependant son but. Les règles de l'art sont un calcul de probabilités sur les moyens de réussir; et si le succès est obtenu, il importe peu de s'y être soumis. Mais il n'en est pas de même du goût; car se mettre au-dessus de lui, c'est s'écarter de la beauté même de la nature; et il n'y a rien au-dessus d'elle.

Ne disons donc pas que Shakespear a su se passer de goût, et se montrer supérieur à ses loix. Reconnoissons, au contraire, qu'il a du goût quand il est sublime, et qu'il manque de goût quand son talent foiblit.

(*De la Littérature*, chapters 11 and 12, vol. 1, pp. 178–92.)

*   *   *   *   *

The name *romantic* has recently been introduced into Germany as a term referring to the poetry that has its origins in the songs of the troubadours, and that is rooted in the traditions of chivalry and Christianity. Unless one concedes that the literary realm is divided between paganism and Christianity, the North and the South, Antiquity and the Middle Ages, chivalry and Greek and Roman institutions, one will never attain a philosophical understanding of ancient as against modern taste.

The word classical is often taken as synonymous with perfection. I use the term here in a different sense, regarding classical poetry as that of the ancients, and romantic poetry as that which in some way adheres to chivalric traditions. This division also coincides with two historical eras: that which preceded the establishment of Christianity, and that which followed it.

In various German works ancient poetry has been compared to sculpture and romantic poetry to painting; the progress of the human spirit has also been characterised in diverse ways as passing from materialistic to spiritualistic religions, from nature to the divine.

The French nation, the most cultured of all Latin nations, inclines towards classical poetry imitated from the Greeks and Romans. The English nation, the most illustrious of the Germanic nations, likes romantic and chivalric poetry, and glories in the masterpieces of this kind that it possesses. I shall not examine here which of the two kinds of poetry merits preference: it suffices to show that the diversity of tastes in this regard devolves not merely from chance causes, but also from basic sources of imagination and thought.

In the epic poems and tragedies of the ancients, there is a sort of simplicity that stems from the fact that mankind at that period identified with nature and believed in its dependence on destiny, like nature's own dependence on necessity. With little reflection, man always externalised his inner state; consciousness itself was represented by external objects, and the torches of the Furies brought remorse upon the heads of the guilty. In ancient times happenings were all-important, character is more prominent in modern times; that gnawing reflection that often devours us, like Prometheus' vulture, would merely have seemed a folly in the clear and precise framework of the social and political conditions of the ancients.

At the dawn of Greek art, only isolated statues were made; the groups were composed later. One could even truthfully maintain that in all the arts no arrangements existed; the objects represented followed one another like the figures in bas-reliefs, without combinations or complications of any kind. Man made nature personal; nymphs inhabited streams, hamadryads dwelt in the forests: but nature in turn took possession of man till he resembled, as it were, the torrent, the thunder, the volcano, so involuntary were his actions and so little modified by reflection in either motive or outcome. The ancients had, so to speak, a corporeal soul, whose impulses were strong, direct and consistent – totally unlike the human heart fostered by Christianity; from Christian repentance the moderns have derived the habit of continual introspection.

But to body forth this wholly internal life, great variety is needed in the details to present the infinite nuances of what transpires in the soul. If nowadays the fine arts were to be confined to the simplicity of the ancients, we would not achieve their distinctive primal force, and we would forfeit those deep and complex emotions inherent in our souls. With the moderns, simplicity in art could easily turn to coldness and abstraction, whereas with the ancients it had been full of life. Honour and love, gallantry and pity are the hallmarks of the age of chivalric

Christianity; and these states can clearly be seen in the dangers, exploits, loves, misfortunes, in short the romantic interest of endlessly varying tableaux. The sources of the artistic effects are, therefore, in many respects different in classical and romantic poetry; in the former it is fate that reigns; in the latter it is Providence; fate does not reckon with the feelings of men, Providence judges their actions solely according to their sentiments. How could poetry not create an entirely different world when it must portray, on the one hand, the workings of a blind and deaf destiny, always in strife with mortals, and on the other, that intelligible order over which a supreme being presides, who is accessible and responsive to our heart!

Pagan poetry must be as simple and striking as outer objects; Christian poetry needs the thousand colours of the rainbow so as not to be lost in the clouds. The poetry of the ancients is purer as art, that of the moderns provokes more tears; but the choice facing us is not between classical and modern poetry, but rather between the imitation of the one and the inspiration of the other. The literature of Antiquity is for us moderns a transplanted literature: romantic or chivalric literature is indigenous to us, for it is our religion and our institutions that have nurtured it. Writers who imitate the ancients have submitted to the most stringent rules of taste; for, unable to rely on their own nature or their own experiences, they had to conform to the laws by which the masterpieces of Antiquity can be adapted to our own taste, even though all the political and religious circumstances which produced these masterpieces have since changed. But these works based on Antiquity, however perfect in themselves, are rarely popular because they have no national grounding in the present.

French poetry, the most classical of all modern poetry, is the only one not widely known among the people. Tasso's stanzas are sung by Venetian gondoliers, the Spanish and Portuguese of all classes know verses of Calderon and Camoens by heart, Shakespeare is just as admired by the common people of

England as by the upper class. Poems by Goethe and Bürger have been set to music and are sung from the banks of the Rhine to the Baltic. Our French poets are admired by all the cultured minds in our country as in the rest of Europe, but they are completely unknown to the ordinary people and even to the urban bourgeoisie because the arts in France are not, as elsewhere, native to the country in which their beauties are unfolded.

Some French critics have claimed that the literature of the Germanic peoples was still in its infancy; this opinion is altogether false: those most versed in the languages and works of the ancients are certainly not unaware of the drawbacks and advantages of the style they adopt or of that they reject; but their character, their habits and their reasoning have led them to prefer a literature founded on recollections of chivalry, the wonders of the Middle Ages, to that based on Greek and Roman mythology. Romantic literature is the only literature still capable of being perfected; as its roots are in our own soil, it is the only art form that can grow and flourish anew; it reflects our religion; it echoes our history; it is old but not ancient in origin.

Classical poetry must filter through memories of paganism to reach us. The poetry of the Germans is the Christian era of the fine arts: it uses our personal experiences to move us: the genius inspiring it speaks directly to our hearts, and seems to evoke our very lives like the most overpowering and dreaded of spirits.

Le nom de *romantique* a été introduit nouvellement en Allemagne pour désigner la poésie dont les chants des troubadours ont été l'origine, celle qui est née de la chevalerie et du christianisme. Si l'on n'admet pas que le paganisme et le christianisme, le nord et le midi, l'antiquité et le moyen âge, la chevalerie et les institutions grecques et romaines, se sont partagé l'empire de la littérature, l'on ne parviendra jamais à juger sous un point de vue philosophique le goût antique et le goût moderne.

On prend quelquefois le mot classique comme synonyme de perfection. Je m'en sers ici dans une autre acception, en considérant la poésie classique comme celle des anciens, et la poésie romantique comme celle qui tient de quelque manière aux traditions chevaleresques. Cette division se rapporte également aux deux ères du monde: celle qui a précédé l'établissement du christianisme, et celle qui l'a suivi.

On a comparé aussi dans divers ouvrages allemands la poésie antique à la sculpture, et la poésie romantique à la peinture; enfin on a caractérisé de toutes les manières la marche de l'esprit humain, passant des religions matérialistes aux religions spiritualistes, de la nature à la divinité.

La nation française, la plus cultivée des nations latines, penche vers la poésie classique imitée des Grecs et des Romains. La nation anglaise, la plus illustre des nations germaniques, aime la poésie romantique et chevaleresque, et se glorifie des chefs-d'œuvre qu'elle possède en ce genre. Je n'examinerai point ici lequel de ces deux genres de poésie mérite la préférence: il suffit de montrer que la diversité des goûts, à cet égard, dérive non-seulement de causes accidentelles, mais aussi des sources primitives de l'imagination et de la pensée.

Il y a dans les poëmes épiques, et dans les tragédies des anciens, un genre de simplicité qui tient à ce que les hommes étoient identifiés à cette époque avec la nature, et croyoient dépendre du destin comme elle dépend de la nécessité. L'homme, réfléchissant peu, portoit toujours l'action de son âme au dehors; la conscience elle-même étoit figurée par des objets extérieurs, et les flambeaux des Furies secouoient les remords sur la tête des coupables. L'événement étoit tout dans l'antiquité, le caractère tient plus de place dans les temps modernes; et cette réflexion inquiète, qui nous dévore souvent comme le vautour de Prométhée, n'eût semblé que de la folie au milieu des rapports clairs et prononcés qui existoient dans l'état civil et social des anciens.

On ne faisoit en Grèce, dans le commencement de l'art, que

des statues isolées, les groupes ont été composés plus tard. On pourroit dire de même, avec vérité, que dans tous les arts il n'y avoit point de groupes; les objets représentés se succédoient comme dans les bas-reliefs, sans combinaison, sans complication d'aucun genre. L'homme personnifioit la nature; des nymphes habitoient les eaux, des hamadryades les forêts: mais la nature à son tour s'emparoit de l'homme, et l'on eût dit qu'il ressembloit au torrent, à la foudre, au volcan, tant il agissoit par une impulsion involontaire, et sans que la réflexion pût en rien altérer les motifs ni les suites de ses actions. Les anciens avoient pour ainsi dire une âme corporelle, dont tous les mouvements étoient forts, directs et conséquents, il n'en est pas de même du cœur humain développé par le christianisme: les modernes ont puisé, dans le repentir chrétien, l'habitude de se replier continuellement sur eux-mêmes.

Mais, pour manifester cette existence toute intérieure, il faut qu'une grande variété dans les faits présente sous toutes les formes les nuances infinies de ce qui se passe dans l'âme. Si de nos jours les beaux-arts étoient astreints à la simplicité des anciens, nous n'atteindrions pas à la force primitive qui les distingue, et nous perdrions les émotions intimes et multipliées dont notre âme est susceptible. La simplicité de l'art, chez les modernes, tourneroit facilement à la froideur et à l'abstraction, tandis que celle des anciens étoit pleine de vie. L'honneur et l'amour, la bravoure et la pitié sont les sentiments qui signalent le christianisme chevaleresque; et ces dispositions de l'âme ne peuvent se faire voir que par les dangers, les exploits, les amours, les malheurs, l'intérêt romantique enfin, qui varie sans cesse les tableaux. Les sources des effets de l'art sont donc différentes à beaucoup d'égards dans la poésie classique et dans la poésie romantique; dans l'une, c'est le sort qui règne; dans l'autre, c'est la Providence; le sort ne compte pour rien les sentiments des hommes, la Providence ne juge les actions que d'après les sentiments. Comment la poésie ne créeroit-elle pas un monde d'une toute autre nature, quand il faut peindre l'œuvre d'un destin aveugle et sourd, toujours en lutte avec les mortels, ou cet ordre intelligent auquel préside un être suprême, que notre cœur interroge, et qui répond à notre cœur!

La poésie païenne doit être simple et saillante comme les objets extérieurs; la poésie chrétienne a besoin des mille couleurs de l'arc-en-ciel pour ne pas se perdre dans les nuages. La poésie des anciens est plus pure comme art, celle des modernes fait verser plus de larmes: mais la question pour nous n'est pas entre la poésie classique et la poésie romantique, mais entre l'imitation de l'une et l'inspiration de l'autre. La littérature des anciens est chez les modernes une littérature transplantée: la littérature romantique ou chevaleresque est chez nous indigène, et c'est notre religion et nos institutions qui l'ont fait éclore. Les écrivains imitateurs des anciens se sont soumis aux règles du goût les plus sévères; car ne pouvant consulter ni leur propre nature, ni leurs propres souvenirs, il a fallu qu'ils se conformassent aux lois d'après lesquelles les chefs-d'œuvre des anciens peuvent être adaptés à notre goût, bien que toutes les circonstances politiques et religieuses qui ont donné le jour à ces chefs-d'œuvre soient changées. Mais ces poésies d'après l'antique, quelque parfaites qu'elles soient, sont rarement populaires, parce qu'elles ne tiennent, dans le temps actuel, à rien de national.

La poésie française étant la plus classique de toutes les poésies modernes, elle est la seule qui ne soit pas répandue parmi le peuple. Les stances du Tasse sont chantées par les gondoliers de Venise, les Espagnols et les Portugais de toutes les classes savent par cœur les vers de Calderon et de Camoëns. Shakespear est autant admiré par le peuple en Angleterre que par la classe supérieure. Des poëmes de Goethe et de Bürger sont mis en musique, et vous les entendez répéter des bords du Rhin jusqu'à la Baltique. Nos poëtes français sont admirés par tout ce qu'il y a d'esprits cultivés chez nous et dans le reste de l'Europe; mais ils sont tout-à-fait inconnus aux gens du peuple et aux bourgeois même des villes, parce que les arts en France ne sont pas comme ailleurs, natifs du pays même où leurs beautés se développent.

Quelques critiques français ont prétendu que la littérature des peuples germaniques étoit encore dans l'enfance de l'art; cette opinion est tout-à-fait fausse: les hommes les plus instruits dans la connoissance des langues et des ouvrages des anciens n'ignorent certainement pas les inconvénients et les avantages du genre qu'ils adoptent ou de celui qu'ils rejettent: mais leur caractère, leurs habitudes et leurs raisonnements les ont conduits à préférer la littérature fondée sur les souvenirs de la chevalerie, sur le merveilleux du moyen âge, à celle dont la mythologie des Grecs est la base. La littérature romantique est la seule qui soit susceptible encore d'être perfectionnée, parce qu'ayant ses racines dans notre propre sol, elle est la seule qui puisse croître et se vivifier de nouveau; elle exprime notre religion; elle rappelle notre histoire: son origine est ancienne, mais non antique.

La poésie classique doit passer par les souvenirs du paganisme pour arriver jusqu'à nous: la poésie des Germains est l'ère chrétienne des beaux-arts: elle se sert de nos impressions personnelles pour nous émouvoir: le génie qui l'inspire s'adresse immédiatement à notre cœur, et semble évoquer notre vie elle-même comme un fantôme le plus puissant et le plus terrible de tous.

(*De L'Allemagne*, chapter 11, *De la Poésie Classique et de la Poésie Romantique*, vol. II, pp. 127–40.)

CLASSICAL VERSUS ROMANTIC

AUGUST WILHELM SCHLEGEL

The whole play of vital motion hinges on harmony and contrast. Why should this phenomenon not also recur on a grander scale in the history of mankind? Perhaps in this notion the true key could be found to the ancient and modern history of poetry and the fine arts. Those who have accepted this have invented for the particular spirit of modern art, in contrast to ancient or classical, the name 'romantic'. The term is certainly not inappropriate. The word is derived from romance, the appellation originally given to the popular languages, which were formed from the mingling of Latin and the old Teutonic dialects, just as modern civilisation is the outcome of the fusion of the alien elements of the northern tribes with fragments of Antiquity, in contrast to the civilisation of the Ancients which was much more of a piece.

Das ganze Spiel lebendiger Bewegung beruht auf Einstimmung und Gegensatz. Warum sollte sich diese Erscheinung nicht auch in der Geschichte der Menschheit im Grossen wiederholen? Vielleicht wäre mit diesem Gedanken der wahre Schlüssel zur alten und neuen Geschichte der Poesie und der schönen Künste gefunden. Die, welche dies annahmen, haben für den eigentümlichen Geist der modernen Kunst, im Gegensatz mit der antiken oder klassischen, den Namen 'romantisch' erfunden. Allerdings nicht unpassend. Das Wort kommt her von romance, der Benennung der Volkssprachen, welche sich durch die Vermischung des Lateinischen mit den Mundarten des Altdeutschen gebildet hatten, gerade wie die neuere Bildung aus den fremdartigen Bestandteilen der nordischen Stammesart und der Bruchstücke des Altertums zusammengeschmolzen ist, da hingegen die Bildung der Alten weit mehr aus einem Stücke war.

(*Vorlesungen über dramatische Kunst und Literatur,*
Kritische Schriften, vol. v, p. 21.)

*   *   *   *   *

Among the Greeks human nature was self-sufficient; it was conscious of no defects, and strove for no other perfection than that which it could actually attain through its own powers. A

higher wisdom teaches us that mankind, through a great trans-
gression, forfeited the place to which it was originally destined,
and that the whole aim of its earthly existence is to strive to
regain that lost position, which it can never achieve on its own.
The old sensual religion sought only outer, transient blessings;
immortality, so far as it was believed, stood like a shadow in the
dark distance, a faint dream of this bright waking life. In the
Christian view all this has been reversed: the contemplation of
the infinite has destroyed the finite; life has become shadow and
darkness, and only yonder does the eternal day of true being
dawn. Such a religion must awake the vague foreboding, which
slumbers in every feeling heart, into a distinct consciousness,
that the happiness for which we here strive is unattainable; that
no external object can ever entirely satisfy our souls; that all
enjoyment is a fleeting illusion. And when the soul, resting, as it
were, under the willows of exile, breathes out its longing for its
distant home, what else but melancholy can be the key-note of
its songs?

So the poetry of the ancients was the poetry of possession,
ours is that of longing; the former is firmly rooted in the soil of
the present, the latter hovers between recollection and yearning.
Let this not be understood as meaning that everything flows in
one uniform lament, and that the voice of melancholy is always
loudly heard. Just as in the serene framework of Greek culture
the asperity of tragedy was nonetheless possible, so romantic
poetry, springing from the source outlined above, can encom-
pass every mood, even the most joyful; but it will always bear
traces of its origins in some ineffable element. Among the
moderns feeling has become altogether more intense, imagination more ethereal, thought more contemplative. In nature, it is
true, the boundaries run into each other, and things are not as
distinctly separated as they have to be in order to pin down a
concept.

The Greek ideal of humanity was a perfect accord and balance
of all forces, natural harmony. The moderns, on the other hand,

have become conscious of an inner dualism, which precludes such an ideal; hence they strive in their poetry to reconcile and indissolubly fuse the two worlds between which we are torn, the spiritual and the sensual. The sensual impressions are to be hallowed through mysterious union with elevated feelings, while the spiritual is to find in tangible forms a sensual counterpart for its inexpressible perceptions of the infinite.

In Greek art and poetry there is a fundamental unconscious unity of form and matter; in the modern, insofar as it has remained true to its peculiar spirit, a deeper interpenetration of the two is sought as a union of contraries. Greek art fulfilled its aims to perfection; the modern can do justice to its striving for the infinite only by approximation, and is, because of a certain appearance of incompletion, in all the greater danger of being misjudged.

Bei den Griechen war die menschliche Natur selbstgenügsam, sie ahnte keinen Mangel und strebte nach keiner andern Vollkommenheit, als die sie wirklich durch ihre eigenen Kräfte erreichen konnte. Eine höhere Weisheit lehrt uns, die Menschheit habe durch eine grosse Verirrung die ihr ursprünglich bestimmte Stelle eingebüsst, und die ganze Bestimmung ihres irdischen Daseins sei, dahin zurückzustreben, welches sie jedoch, sich selbst überlassen, nicht vermöge. Jene sinnliche Religion wollte nur äussere vergängliche Segnungen erwerben; die Unsterblichkeit, insofern sie geglaubt wurde, stand in dunkler Ferne wie ein Schatten, ein abgeschwächter Traum dieses wachen hellen Lebenstages. In der christlichen Ansicht hat sich alles umgekehrt: die Anschauung des Unendlichen hat das Endliche vernichtet; das Leben ist zur Schattenwelt und zur Nacht geworden, und erst jenseits geht der ewige Tag des wesentlichen Daseins auf. Eine solche Religion muss die Ahnung, die in allen gefühlvollen Herzen schlummert, zum deutlichen Bewusstsein wecken, dass wir nach einer hier unerreichbaren Glückseligkeit trachten, dass kein äusserer Gegenstand jemals unsre Seele ganz

wird erfüllen können, dass aller Genuss eine flüchtige Täuschung ist. Und wenn nun die Seele, gleichsam unter den
Trauerweiden der Verbannung ruhend, ihr Verlangen nach der
fremd gewordenen Heimat ausatmet, was andres kann der
Grundton ihrer Lieder sein als Schwermut? So ist es denn auch:
die Poesie der Alten war die des Besitzes, die unsrige ist die der
Sehnsucht; jene steht fest auf dem Boden der Gegenwart, diese
wiegt sich zwischen Erinnerung und Ahnung. Man missver-
stehe dies nicht, als ob alles in einförmige Klage verfliessen und
die Melancholie sich immer vorlaut aussprechen müsste. Wie in
der heitern Weltansicht der Griechen die herbe Tragödie
dennoch möglich war, so kann auch die aus der oben geschilder-
ten entsprungene romantische Poesie alle Stimmungen bis zur
fröhlichsten durchgehen; aber sie wird immer in einem namen-
losen Etwas Spuren ihrer Quelle an sich tragen. Das Gefühl ist
im Ganzen bei den Neueren inniger, die Phantasie unkörper-
licher, der Gedanke beschaulicher geworden. Freilich laufen in
der Natur die Grenzen ineinander, und die Dinge scheiden sich
nicht so strenge, als man es tun muss, um einen Begriff festzuhalten.

Das griechische Ideal der Menschheit war vollkommene Ein-
tracht und Ebenmass aller Kräfte, natürliche Harmonie. Die
Neueren hingegen sind zum Bewusstsein der inneren
Entzweiung gekommen, welche ein solches Ideal unmöglich
macht; daher ist das Streben ihrer Poesie, diese beiden Welten,
zwischen denen wir uns geteilt fühlen, die geistige und sinnliche, miteinander auszusöhnen und unauflöslich zu verschmelzen. Die sinnlichen Eindrücke sollen durch ihr geheimnisvolles Bündnis mit höheren Gefühlen gleichsam geheiligt
werden, der Geist hingegen will seine Ahnungen oder unnenn-
baren Anschauungen vom Unendlichen in der sinnlichen Erscheinung sinnbildlich niederlegen.

In der griechischen Kunst und Poesie ist ursprüngliche
bewusstlose Einheit der Form und des Stoffes; in der neueren,
sofern sie ihrem eigentümlichen Geist treu geblieben, wird

innigere Durchdringung beider als zweier Entgegengesetzten gesucht. Jene hat ihre Aufgabe bis zur Vollendung gelöst; diese kann ihrem Streben ins Unendliche hin nur durch Annäherung Genüge leisten und ist wegen eines gewissen Scheins von Unvollendung umso eher in Gefahr, verkannt zu werden.

(*Vorlesungen über dramatische Kunst und Literatur*, *Kritische Schriften*, vol. v, pp. 25–6.)

POETRY OF THE SUPERNATURAL

SAMUEL TAYLOR COLERIDGE

During the first year that Mr Wordsworth and I were neighbours, our conversations turned frequently on the two cardinal points of poetry, the power of exciting the sympathy of the reader by a faithful adherence to the truth of nature, and the power of giving the interest of novelty by the modifying colours of imagination. The sudden charm, which accidents of light and shade, which moon-light or sun-set diffused over a known and familiar landscape, appeared to represent the practicability of combining both. These are the poetry of nature. The thought suggested itself (to which of us I do not recollect) that a series of poems might be composed of two sorts. In the one, the incidents and agents were to be, in part at least, supernatural; and the excellence aimed at was to consist in the interesting of the affections by the dramatic truth of such emotions, as would naturally accompany such situations, supposing them real. And real in *this* sense they have been to every human being who, from whatever source of delusion, has at any time believed himself under supernatural agency. For the second class, subjects were to be chosen from ordinary life; the characters and incidents were to be such, as will be found in every village and its vicinity, where there is a meditative and feeling mind to seek after them, or to notice them, when they present themselves.

In this idea originated the plan of the 'Lyrical Ballads'; in which it was agreed, that my endeavours should be directed to persons and characters supernatural, or at least romantic; yet so as to transfer from our inward nature a human interest and a semblance of truth sufficient to procure from these shadows of imagination that willing suspension of disbelief for the moment, which constitutes poetic faith. Mr Wordsworth, on the other hand, was to propose to himself as his object, to give the charm of novelty to things of every day, and to excite a feeling analogous to the supernatural, by awakening the mind's attention from the lethargy of custom, and directing it to the loveliness and the wonders of the world before us; an inexhaustible treasure, but for which, in consequence of the film of familiarity and selfish solicitude we have eyes, yet see not, ears that hear not, and hearts that neither feel nor understand.

(*Biographia Literaria*, chapter 14, vol. II, pp. 5–6.)

POETRY OF THE IMAGINATION

PERCY BYSSHE SHELLEY

According to one mode of regarding those two classes of mental action, which are called reason and imagination, the former may be considered as mind contemplating the relations borne by one thought to another, however produced; and the latter, as mind acting upon those thoughts so as to colour them with its own light, and composing from them, as from elements, other thoughts, each containing within itself the principle of its own integrity. The one is the τὸ ποιεῖν, or the principle of synthesis, and has for its objects those forms which are common to universal nature and existence itself; the other is the τὸ λογίζειν, or principle of analysis, and its action regards the relations of things, simply as relations; considering thoughts, not in their integral unity, but as the algebraical representations which conduct to certain general results. Reason is the enumeration of quantities already known; imagination is the perception of the value of those quantities, both separately and as a whole. Reason respects the differences, and imagination the similitudes of things. Reason is to imagination as the instrument to the agent, as the body to the spirit, as the shadow to the substance.

Poetry, in a general sense, may be defined to be 'the expression of the imagination': and poetry is connate with the origin of man. Man is an instrument over which a series of external and internal impressions are driven, like the alternations of an ever-changing wind over an Aeolian lyre, which move it by their motion to ever-changing melody. But there is a principle within the human being, and perhaps within all sentient beings, which acts otherwise than in the lyre, and produces not melody, alone, but harmony, by an internal adjustment of the sounds or motions thus excited to the impressions which excite them. It is as if the lyre could accommodate its chords to the motions of that which strikes them, in a determined proportion of sound; even as the musician can accommodate his voice to the sound of the lyre. A child at play by itself will express its delight by its voice and motions; and every inflexion of tone and every gesture will bear exact relation to a corresponding antitype in the pleasurable impressions which awakened it; it will be the reflected image of that impression; and as the lyre trembles and sounds after the wind has died away, so the child seeks, by prolonging in its voice and motions the duration of the effect, to prolong also a consciousness of the cause. In relation to the objects which delight a child, these expressions are, what poetry is to higher objects. The savage (for the savage is to ages what the child is to years) expresses the emotions produced in him by surrounding objects in a similar manner; and language and gesture, together with plastic or pictorial imitation, become the image of the combined effect of those objects, and of his apprehension of them. Man in society, with all his passions and his pleasures, next becomes the object of the passions and pleasures of man; an additional class of emotions produces an augmented treasure of expressions; and language, gesture, and the imitative arts, become at once the representation and the medium, the pencil and the picture, the chisel and the statue, the chord and the harmony. The social sympathies, or those laws from which, as from its elements, society results, begin to develop themselves from the moment that two human beings coexist; the future is contained within the present, as the plant within the seed; and equality, diversity, unity, contrast, mutual dependence, become the principles alone capable of affording the motives according to which the will of a social being is determined to action, inasmuch as he is social; and constitute pleasure in sensation, virtue in sentiment, beauty in art, truth in reasoning, and love in the intercourse of kind.

(*A Defence of Poetry*, *Complete Works*, vol. VII,
pp. 109–10.)

ROMANTIC AS CONTEMPORARY

STENDHAL

Romanticism is the art of offering people the literary works which, in the present state of their customs and beliefs, can give them the greatest pleasure.

Classicism, by contrast, offers them the literature which gave the greatest possible pleasure to their great-grandfathers.

Sophocles and Euripides were eminently romantic; to the Greeks, assembled in the theatre in Athens, they gave tragedies which, in the light of that nation's manners, religion, and concepts of human dignity, surely vouchsafed them the greatest possible pleasure.

To imitate Sophocles and Euripides today, and to pretend that these imitations do not make nineteenth-century French men yawn, that is classicism.

I contend without hesitation that Racine was romantic; to the marquises at the court of Louis XIV he gave a portrayal of passions, tempered by the *extreme dignity* then in vogue, that required a duke of 1670 never to fail, even in the tenderest outpourings of paternal love, to address his son as: *Sir*.

That is why Pylades in *Andromaque* always calls Orestes: *Lord*; but what a close friendship that was!

That sort of dignity is nowhere apparent among the Greeks, and it is because of that *dignity*, which leaves us cold today, that Racine was romantic.

Shakespeare was romantic because he proffered to the English of 1590 first the bloody calamities of the civil wars, and then, as a respite from these sad sights, a host of subtle portrayals of the stirrings of the heart, the most delicate shades of passion.

Le *romanticisme* est l'art de présenter aux peuples les œuvres littéraires qui, dans l'état actuel de leurs habitudes et de leurs croyances, sont susceptibles de leur donner le plus de plaisir possible.

Le *classicisme*, au contraire, leur présente la littérature qui donnait le plus grand plaisir possible à leurs arrière-grands-pères.

Sophocle et Euripide furent éminemment romantiques; ils donnèrent, aux Grecs rassemblés au théâtre d'Athènes, les tragédies qui, d'après les habitudes morales de ce peuple, sa religion, ses préjugés sur ce qui fait la dignité de l'homme, devaient lui procurer le plus grand plaisir possible.

Imiter aujourd'hui Sophocle et Euripide, et prétendre que ces imitations ne feront pas bâiller le Français du dix-neuvième siècle, c'est du classicisme.

Je n'hésite pas à avancer que Racine a été romantique; il a donné, aux marquis de la cour de Louis XIV, une peinture des passions, tempérée par l'*extrême dignité* qui alors était de mode, et qui faisait qu'un duc de 1670, même dans les épanchements les plus tendres de l'amour paternel, ne manquait jamais d'appeler son fils: *Monsieur*.

C'est pour cela que le Pylade d''*Andromaque*' dit toujours à Oreste: *Seigneur*; et cependant quelle amitié que celle d'Oreste et de Pylade!

Cette dignité-là n'est nullement dans les Grecs, et c'est à cause de cette *dignité*, qui nous glace aujourd'hui, que Racine a été romantique.

Shakespeare fut romantique parce qu'il présenta aux Anglais de l'an 1590, d'abord les catastrophes sanglantes amenées par les guerres civiles, et, pour reposer de ces tristes spectacles, une foule de peintures fines des mouvements du cœur, et des nuances de passions les plus délicates.

(*Racine et Shakespeare*, part 1, chapter 3, 'Ce que c'est que le romanticisme', pp. 62–3.)

*   *   *   *   *

Molière was a romantic in 1670, since the court was full of Orontes, and the provincial castles were peopled with malcontent Alcestes. To put it plainly, ALL THE GREAT WRITERS HAVE BEEN ROMANTICS IN THEIR TIME. A century after their death, it is those who copy them, instead of opening their eyes and imitating nature, who are classicists.

Molière était romantique en 1670, car la cour était peuplée d'Orontes, et les châteaux de province d'Alcestes fort mécontents. A le bien prendre, TOUS LES GRANDS ÉCRIVAINS ONT ÉTÉ ROMANTIQUES DE LEUR TEMPS. C'est, un siècle après leur mort, les gens qui copient au lieu d'ouvrir les yeux et d'imiter la nature, qui sont classiques.

(*Racine et Shakespeare*, part 2, 'Réponse – Le Romantique au Classique', pp. 118–19.)

PROTEST AND REVOLT

VICTOR HUGO

Romanticism, so often ill defined, is in the final analysis, and here is its real definition, if one considers only its militant aspect, nothing other than liberalism in literature.

Le romantisme, tant de fois mal défini, n'est, à tout prendre, et c'est là sa définition réelle, si l'on ne l'envisage que sous son côté militant, que le libéralisme en littérature.

(Preface to *Hernani*, p. 30.)

*   *   *   *   *

DUVERGIER DE HAURANNE

To sum up, obedience to the rules of language, independence in all other matters: that should be the basic slogan of the romantics; that is the flag they oppose to the one bearing in huge letters the words *intolerance* and *routine*: the future will show which is the better.

En un mot, asservissement aux règles de la langue, indépendance pour tout le reste: telle doit être au moins la devise des romantiques; tel est le drapeau qu'ils opposent à celui qui porte en grosses lettres les mots *intolérance* et *routine*: l'avenir dira lequel est le meilleur.

(*Le Globe*, 24 March 1825; *Le Romantisme défini par 'Le Globe'*, ed. P. Trahard, p. 13.)

*   *   *   *   *

LUDOVIC VITET

Nearly forty years ago a great revolution came, bringing us almost all the freedoms we were claiming. Our social order and customs have taken on new life, industry and thought have been liberated, government moderated; to put it briefly, the philosophers have won their case: but the case they had neglected to present is still undecided, the parties still face each other in the courtroom, and the verdict is still awaited. In fact, the outcome is not in doubt, for each day literary reform sees the ranks of its partisans increasing, although its victory is not yet confirmed; taste in France still awaits its *fourteenth of July*.

To prepare for this new revolution, new encyclopedists have appeared; they are called *Romantics*. Inheritors, not of the doctrines, but of the role of their predecessors, they plead for that independence that has too long been neglected, but that nonetheless is the necessary complement to individual freedom: independence in matters of taste. Their task is confined to claiming for every Frenchman of reason and feeling the right to enjoy what pleases him, to be moved by what moves him, to admire what seems to him admirable, even when it could be proved to him, by well and duly established principles, that he ought not to admire it, or be moved by it, or enjoy it.

Such is romanticism for those who understand it in its widest and most general sense, or rather, from a philosophical angle. *It is, in a nutshell, protestantism in the arts and letters.*

Voici bientôt quarante ans qu'une grande révolution est venue nous apporter presque toutes les libertés que nous réclamions. Notre ordre social et nos mœurs ont été rajeunis, l'industrie et la pensée affranchies, le gouvernement mitigé; en un mot, les philosophes ont gagné leur procès: mais la cause qu'ils avaient oublié d'instruire est encore en suspens, les parties sont encore en présence, et le jugement se fait attendre. A la vérité l'issue n'est pas douteuse, chaque jour la réforme littéraire voit grossir les rangs de ses partisans, mais son triomphe n'est pas encore consacré, le goût en France attend son *14 juillet*.

Pour préparer cette nouvelle révolution, de nouveaux encyclopédistes se sont élevés; on les appelle *Romantiques*. Héritiers, non des doctrines, mais du rôle de leurs devanciers, ils plaident pour cette indépendance trop long-temps négligée, et qui pourtant est le complément nécessaire de la liberté individuelle, l'indépendance en matière de goût. Leur tâche se borne à réclamer pour tout Français doué de raison et de sentiment le droit de s'amuser de ce qui lui fait plaisir, de s'émouvoir de ce qui l'émeut, d'admirer ce qui lui semble admirable, lors même qu'en vertu des principes bien et dûment consacrés, on pourrait lui prouver qu'il ne doit ni admirer, ni s'émouvoir, ni s'amuser.

Tel est le romantisme pour ceux qui le comprennent dans son acception la plus large et la plus générale, ou pour mieux dire, d'une manière philosophique. *C'est, en deux mots, le protestantisme dans les lettres et les arts.*

(*Le Globe*, 2 April, 1825; *Le Romantisme défini par 'Le Globe'*, ed. P. Trahard, pp. 20–1.)

*   *   *   *   *

Thus, strictly speaking, *romanticism is, in practice, a lively coalition of diverse interests, but with a common goal, warfare against the rules, the rules of convention.*

Ainsi, à proprement parler, *le romantisme pratique est une coalition animée d'intérêts divers, mais qui a un but commun, la guerre aux règles, aux règles de convention.*

(*Le Globe*, 2 April, 1825; *Le Romantisme défini par 'Le Globe'*, ed. P. Trahard, p. 24.)

WHAT IS ROMANTICISM, AFTER ALL?

ALFRED DE MUSSET

I was telling you that we didn't understand what this word *romanticism* meant. If my tale at first strikes you as old and familiar, don't take fright, just let me go on, I mean – to come to a conclusion. It was about 1824, or a little later – I forget; a controversy was raging in the *Journal des Débats*. It was about the *picturesque*, the *grotesque*, the description of landscape in poetry, the dramatisation of history, censured drama, pure art, broken rhythm, the mingling of the tragic with the comic, and the revival of the Middle Ages.

[. . .]

However, Cotonet and I decided to look into the matter more deeply, and to come to grips with the schisms polarising so many sprightly minds. We were well schooled. Specially Cotonet, who is a notary and whose hobby is ornithology. We believed at the outset, for two whole years, that *romanticism* in literature was applicable only to the theatre, and that it differed from the classical in doing without the unities.

[. . .]

But suddenly (about 1828, I think) we are told that there is romantic and classical poetry, a romantic and a classical novel, a romantic and a classical ode; indeed, a single line, my dear Sir, a single line all alone can be romantic or classical, according to its fancy.

When we heard this, we couldn't sleep at night. Two years of peaceful certainty had evaporated like a dream. All our ideas were upset; for if Aristotle's rules were no longer the line of demarcation between the literary camps, where was one to take one's bearings and on what was one to rely? Reading a work, how was one to know to which school it belonged? We did think that the experts in Paris must have some formula that promptly solved the problem; but what was one to do in the provinces? And I must tell you, sir, that in the provinces the word *romantic* generally has a meaning easy to grasp: it is synonymous with absurd, and no one bothers about it. Fortunately, a famous preface appeared that same year, which we immediately devoured and which almost convinced us for good and all. It exuded an air of confidence, as if made to set one's mind at rest, and it explained the principles of the new school in great detail. It said quite clearly, that romanticism was nothing other than the combination of the zaney and the serious, the grotesque and the terrible, the farcical and the horrible, or, if you prefer, comedy and tragedy.

[. . .]

So there we were, Cotonet and I, once again lapsed into uncertainty. Romanticism must surely be, if not a recent, at least a modern discovery. It was not, then, a combination of the comic and the tragic, nor the flaunting of Aristotle's rules (I forgot to tell you that Aristophanes himself did not heed the unities). Our reasoning was quite simple: 'Since there are disputes in Paris in the theatres, the prefaces and the newspapers, they must be about something; since authors are announcing a real find, a new art and a new faith, then this thing must be more than a mere revival from the Greeks; and since we have nothing better to do, we are going to ferret out what it is.'

[. . .]

And, on the subject of new words, I will confess to you that for another whole year we fell into a sad error. Weary of analysing and pondering, finding always empty phrases and incomprehensible professions of faith, we came to believe that this word *romanticism* was no more than a word; we thought it beautiful, and it seemed a pity that it meant nothing.

[. . .]

Until 1830 we believed that romanticism was imitation of the Germans, to whom we added the English, upon advice given to us.

[. . .]

Could the classical then be only the imitation of Greek poetry, and the romantic only the imitation of German, English and Spanish poetry? The devil take it! what would then become of all those fine treatises on Boileau and Aristotle, Antiquity and Christianity, genius and liberty, the past and the future, etc.? It couldn't possibly be; that couldn't be the outcome of our eager and assiduous research. We wondered, could it be only a matter of form? This impenetrable romanticism, could it lie in the broken line in verse, about which so much fuss is made? But no; for in their arguments we see the new authors referring to Molière and others as having set the example for this technique; besides, the broken line in verse is horrible, indeed wicked; it is a sacrilege, an affront to the Muse.

I am naively expounding to you, sir, the whole sequence of our tribulations, and if you find my tale rather long, you must bear in mind twelve years of suffering; we are making progress, don't worry. From 1830 to 1831, we believed that romanticism was the historical mode.

[. . .]

From 1831 to the following year, seeing the historical mode in disrepute and romanticism still alive, we thought it was the *intimate* manner, that was being much discussed.

[. . .]

From 1832 to 1833, it occurred to us that romanticism could be a system of philosophy and political economy.

[. . .]

From 1833 to 1834, we believed that romanticism meant not shaving and wearing waistcoats with large lapels starched stiff. The following year we believed it meant refusing to go on guard. The following year we believed nothing, for Cotonet had gone to the South to see about an inheritance, and I myself was very busy mending a barn damaged by the heavy rains.

Je vous disais que nous ne comprenions pas ce que signifiait ce mot de *romantisme*. Si ce que je vous raconte vous paraît un peu usé et connu au premier abord, il ne faut pas vous effrayer, mais seulement me laisser faire; j'ai l'intention d'en venir à mes fins. C'était donc vers 1824, ou un peu plus tard, je l'ai oublié; on se battait dans le *Journal des Débats*. Il était question de *pittoresque*, de *grotesque*, du paysage introduit dans la poésie, de l'histoire dramatisée, du drame blasonné, de l'art pur, du

rythme brisé, du tragique fondu avec le comique, et du moyen
âge ressuscité.

[. . .]

Cependant, Cotonet et moi, nous résolûmes d'approfondir la
question, et de nous rendre compte des querelles qui divisaient
tant d'esprits habiles. Nous avons fait de bonnes études,
Cotonet surtout, qui est notaire et qui s'occupe d'ornithologie.
Nous crûmes d'abord, pendant deux ans, que le *romantisme*, en
matière d'écriture, ne s'appliquait qu'au théâtre, et qu'il se
distinguait du classique parce qu'il se passait des unités.

[. . .]

Mais on nous apprend tout à coup (c'était, je crois, en 1828)
qu'il y avait poésie romantique et poésie classique, roman
romantique et roman classique, ode romantique et ode
classique; que dis-je? un seul vers, mon cher monsieur, un seul
et unique vers pouvait être romantique ou classique, selon que
l'envie lui en prenait.

Quand nous reçûmes cette nouvelle, nous ne pûmes fermer
l'œil de la nuit. Deux ans de paisible conviction venaient de
s'évanouir comme un songe. Toutes nos idées étaient
bouleversées; car si les règles d'Aristote n'étaient plus la ligne de
démarcation qui séparait les camps littéraires, où se retrouver et
sur quoi s'appuyer? Par quel moyen, en lisant un ouvrage,
savoir à quel école il appartenait? Nous pensions bien que les
initiés de Paris devaient avoir une espèce de mot d'ordre qui les
tirait d'abord d'embarras; mais en province, comment faire? Et
il faut vous dire, monsieur, qu'en province, le mot *romantique*
a, en général, une signification facile à retenir, il est synonyme
d'absurde, et on ne s'en inquiète pas autrement. Heureusement,
dans la même année, parut une illustre préface que nous
dévorâmes aussitôt, et qui faillit nous convaincre à jamais. Il y
respirait un air d'assurance qui était fait pour tranquilliser, et les
principes de la nouvelle école s'y trouvaient détaillés au long. On
y disait très nettement que le romantisme n'était autre chose que
l'alliance du fou et du sérieux, du grotesque et du terrible, du

bouffon et de l'horrible, autrement dit, si vous l'aimez mieux, de la comédie et de la tragédie.

[. . .]

Nous voilà donc, Cotonet et moi, retombés dans l'incertitude. Le romantisme devait, avant tout, être une découverte, sinon récente, du moins moderne. Ce n'était donc pas plus l'alliance du comique et du tragique que l'infraction permise aux règles d'Aristote (j'ai oublié de vous dire qu'Aristophane ne tient lui-même aucun compte des unités). Nous fîmes donc ce raisonnement très simple: 'Puisqu'on se bat à Paris dans les théâtres, dans les préfaces, et dans les journaux, il faut que ce soit pour quelque chose; puisque les auteurs proclament une trouvaille, un art nouveau et une foi nouvelle, il faut que ce quelque chose soit autre chose qu'une chose renouvelée des Grecs; puisque nous n'avons rien de mieux à faire nous allons chercher ce que c'est.'

*   *   *   *   *

Et, à propos des mots nouveaux, je vous dirai que, durant une autre année, nous tombâmes dans une triste erreur. Las d'examiner et de peser, trouvant toujours des phrases vides et des professions de foi incompréhensibles, nous en vînmes à croire que ce mot de *romantisme* n'était qu'un mot; nous le trouvions beau, et il nous semblait que c'était dommage qu'il ne voulût rien dire.

[. . .]

Nous crûmes, jusqu'en 1830, que le romantisme était l'imitation des Allemands, et nous y ajoutâmes les Anglais, sur le conseil qu'on nous en donna.

[. . .]

Le classique ne serait-il donc que l'imitation de la poésie grecque, et le romantique que l'imitation des poésies allemande, anglaise et espagnole? Diable! que deviendraient alors tant de beaux discours sur Boileau et sur Aristote, sur l'antiquité et le christianisme, sur le génie et la liberté, sur le passé et sur l'avenir, etc. . . . ? C'est impossible; quelque chose nous criait que ce ne pouvait être là le résultat de recherches si curieuses et si empressées. Ne serait-ce pas, pensâmes-nous, seulement affaire de forme? Ce romantisme indéchiffrable ne consisterait-il pas dans ce vers brisé dont on fait assez de bruit dans le monde? Mais non; car, dans leurs plaidoyers, nous voyons les auteurs nouveaux citer Molière et quelques autres comme ayant donné l'exemple de cette méthode; le vers brisé, d'ailleurs, est horrible, il faut dire plus, il est impie; c'est un sacrilège envers les dieux, une offense à la Muse.

Je vous expose naïvement, monsieur, toute la suite de nos tribulations, et si vous trouvez mon récit un peu long, il faut songer à douze ans de souffrances; nous avançons, ne vous inquiétez pas. De 1830 à 1831, nous crûmes que le romantisme était le genre historique.

[. . .]

De 1831 à l'année suivante, voyant le genre historique discrédité, et le romantisme toujours en vie, nous pensâmes que c'était le genre *intime*, dont on parlait fort.

[. . .]

De 1832 à 1833, il nous vint à l'esprit que le romantisme pouvait être un système de philosophie et d'économie politique.

[. . .]

De 1833 à 1834 nous crûmes que le romantisme consistait à ne pas se raser, et à porter des gilets à larges revers, très empesés. L'année suivante, nous crûmes que c'était de refuser de monter la garde. L'année d'après, nous ne crûmes rien, Cotonet ayant fait un petit voyage pour une succession dans le Midi, et me trouvant moi-même très occupé à faire réparer une grange que les grandes pluies m'avaient endommagée.

(*Lettres de Dupuis et Cotonet*, *Œuvres complètes*, vol. III, pp. 820–8.)

PART II

ROMANTIC ART:
THE GUIDING PRINCIPLES

THE FUNCTION OF ART

WILHELM HEINRICH WACKENRODER

I know, however, of two wonderful languages, through which the Creator has granted man the means of grasping and comprehending divine matters in their full force, in so far as that is at all possible for mortal creatures (not to seem presumptuous). These languages speak to our inner selves, but not with the aid of words; suddenly, and in wondrous fashion, they move our whole being, permeating every nerve and every drop of blood in us. One of these wonderful languages is spoken by God alone; the other is spoken by a few chosen among men, whom He has annointed as His favourites. I am referring to: Nature and Art.

[. . .]

Art is a language quite different from nature, but it too, in similarly mysterious and secret ways, exercises a marvellous power over the human heart. Art speaks through pictorial representations of men, and uses a hieroglyphic language, whose signs we recognise and understand through their exterior. But in the visible figures which it presents, the spiritual and the sensuous are merged in such a touching and admirable manner, that the whole of our selves and every fibre of our being is again moved and stirred to the core.

[. . .]

One of these languages, which the Almighty Himself speaks from eternity to eternity, the language of ever living, infinite nature, raises us through the immensities of space directly to the

Divinity himself. Art, however, which by the meaningful combination of coloured earth and a little moisture recreates the
human shape in ideal form within a narrow, limited space (a
kind of creative act that has been granted to mortals) – art opens
up to us the treasures in the human breast, turns our gaze
inwards, and shows us the invisible, I mean all that is noble,
sublime and divine, in human form.

[. . .]

Art represents the highest human perfection. Nature, as far as
it is perceptible to the human eye, is like a fragmentary oracular
utterance from the mouth of the Divinity. If one may speak so
familiarly of such things, one might perhaps say, that God views
the whole realm of nature or the entire universe in the same way
as we see the work of art.

Ich kenne aber zwei wunderbare Sprachen, durch welche der
Schöpfer den Menschen vergönnt hat, die himmlischen Dinge
in ganzer Macht, soviel es nämlich (um nicht verwegen zu
sprechen) sterblichen Geschöpfen möglich ist, zu fassen und zu
begreifen. Sie kommen durch ganz andere Wege zu unserm
Inneren als durch die Hülfe der Worte; sie bewegen auf einmal
auf eine wunderbare Weise unser ganzes Wesen und drängen
sich in jede Nerve und jeden Blutstropfen, der uns angehört.
Die eine dieser wundervollen Sprachen redet nur Gott, die
andere reden nur wenige Auserwählte unter den Menschen, die
er zu seinen Lieblingen gesalbt hat. Ich meine: die Natur und
die Kunst.

[. . .]

Die Kunst ist eine Sprache ganz anderer Art als die Natur;
aber auch ihr ist durch ähnliche dunkle und geheime Wege eine
wunderbare Kraft auf das Herz des Menschen eigen. Sie redet
durch Bilder der Menschen und bedient sich also einer Hieroglyphenschrift, deren Zeichen wir dem Äussern nach kennen
und verstehen. Aber sie schmelzt das Geistige und Sinnliche auf
eine so rührende und bewunderungswürdige Weise in die sicht-

baren Gestalten hinein, dass wiederum unser ganzes Wesen und alles, was an uns ist, von Grund auf bewegt und erschüttert wird.

[. . .]

Die eine der Sprachen, welche der Höchste selber von Ewigkeit zu Ewigkeit fortredet, die ewig lebendige, unendliche Natur, ziehet uns durch die weiten Räume der Lüfte unmittelbar zu der Gottheit hinauf. Die Kunst aber, die durch sinnreiche Zusammensetzungen von gefärbter Erde und etwas Feuchtigkeit die menschliche Gestalt in einem engen, begrenzten Raume, nach innerer Vollendung strebend, nachahmt (eine Art von Schöpfung, wie sie sterblichen Wesen hervorzubringen vergönnt ward) – sie schliesst uns die Schätze in der menschlichen Brust auf, richtet unsern Blick in unser Inneres und zeigt uns das Unsichtbare, ich meine alles, was edel, gross und göttlich ist, in menschlicher Gestalt.

[. . .]

Die Kunst stellet uns die höchste menschliche Vollendung dar. Die Natur, soviel davon ein sterbliches Auge sieht, gleichet abgebrochenen Orakelsprüchen aus dem Munde der Gottheit. Ist es aber erlaubt, also von dergleichen Dingen zu reden, so möchte man vielleicht sagen, dass Gott wohl die ganze Natur oder die ganze Welt auf ähnliche Art, wie wir ein Kunstwerk, ansehen möge.

(Herzensergiessungen eines kunstliebenden Kloster-
bruders, pp. 52–5.)

NOVALIS

Poetry elevates each individual phenomenon through an original association with the rest of the whole – and if philosophy through its positing of laws prepares the world for the effective impact of ideas, then poetry, as it were, is the key to philosophy, its purpose and its significance – for poetry shapes the beautiful social order – the world family – the beautiful establishment of the universe.

Just as philosophy by means of system and state strengthens the forces of the individual through the forces of humanity and the universe, making the whole an organ of the individual and the individual an organ of the whole – so does poetry in relation to life. The individual lives in the whole and the whole in the individual. Through poetry the highest accord and interactivity comes into being, the closest communion between the finite and the infinite.

Die Poesie hebt jedes Einzelne durch eine eigentümliche Verknüpfung mit dem übrigen Ganzen – und wenn die Philosophie durch ihre Gesetzgebung die Welt erst zu dem wirksamen Einfluss der Ideen bereitet, so ist gleichsam Poesie der Schlüssel der Philosophie, ihr Zweck und ihre Bedeutung; denn die Poesie bildet die schöne Gesellschaft – die Weltfamilie – die schöne Haushaltung des Universums.

Wie die Philosophie durch System und Staat die Kräfte des Individuums mit den Kräften der Menschheit und des Weltalls verstärkt, das Ganze zum Organ des Individuums und das Individuum zum Organ des Ganzen macht – so die Poesie in Ansehung des Lebens. Das Individuum lebt im Ganzen und das Ganze im Individuum. Durch Poesie entsteht die höchste Sympathie und Koaktivität, die innigste Gemeinschaft des Endlichen und Unendlichen.

(*Fragmente des Jahres 1798, Gesammelte Werke*, No. 807, vol. III, pp. 22–3.)

*   *   *   *   *

Poetry is the great art of the building of transcendental health. The poet thus is the transcendental doctor.

Poetry shunts and shifts pain and pleasure – desire and aversion – fallacy and truth – health and disease. It intertwines everything for its great purpose of purposes: *the elevation of mankind above itself*.

Poesie ist die grosse Kunst der Konstruktion der transzendentalen Gesundheit. Der Poet ist also der transzendentale Arzt.

Die Poesie schaltet und waltet mit Schmerz und Kitzel – mit Lust und Unlust – Irrtum und Wahrheit – Gesundheit und Krankheit. Sie mischt alles zu ihrem grossen Zweck der Zwecke: *der Erhebung des Menschen über sich selbst*.

> (*Fragmente des Jahres 1798, Gesammelte Werke*, No. 818, vol. III, p. 25.)

*   *   *   *   *

Poetry is the genuine absolute Reality. That is the kernel of my philosophy. The more poetic, the truer.

Die Poesie ist das echt absolut Reele. Dies ist der Kern meiner Philosophie. Je poetischer, je wahrer.

> (*Fragmente des Jahres 1798, Gesammelte Werke*, No. 1247, vol. III, p. 141.)

*   *   *   *   *

Poetry is representation of the spirit – of the inner world in its totality. Its medium already, words, hint at this for they are the outer revelation of that inner realm of power.

Poesie ist Darstellung des Gemüts – der innern Welt in ihrer Gesamtheit. Schon ihr Medium, die Worte, deuten es an, denn sie sind ja die äussre Offenbarung jenes innern Kraftreichs.

> (*Fragmente aus den letzten Jahren 1799–1800, Gesammelte Werke*, No. 2857, vol. IV, p. 256.)

*   *   *   *   *

Should not poetry be nothing other than inner painting, music etc.? Modified, it is true, by the nature of the spirit.

In poetry, which is in a sense only an appropriate mechanical instrument, one seeks to bring forth inner moods and pictures or contemplations, perhaps even spiritual dances etc.

Poetry = the art of moving the spirit.

Sollte Poesie nichts als innre Malerei und Musik etc. sein? Freilich modifiziert durch die Natur des Gemüts.

Man sucht mit der Poesie, die gleichsam nur das mechanische Instrument dazu ist, innre Stimmungen und Gemälde oder Anschauungen hervorzubringen, vielleicht auch geistige Tänze etc.

Poesie = Gemütserregungskunst.

> (*Fragmente aus den letzten Jahren 1799–1800*,
> *Gesammelte Werke*, No. 2907, vol. IV, p. 267.)

*   *   *   *   *

The feeling for poetry has much in common with the feeling for mysticism. It is the feeling for the particular, the personal, the unknown, the arcane, the revelatory, the perforce adventitious. It portrays the unportrayable. It sees the invisible, senses the impalpable.

Der Sinn für Poesie hat viel mit dem Sinn für Mystizismus gemein. Er ist der Sinn für das Eigentümliche, Personelle, Unbekannte, Geheimnisvolle, zu Offenbarende, das Notwendig-Zufällige. Er stellt das Undarstellbare dar. Er sieht das Unsichtbare, fühlt das Unfühlbare.

> (*Fragmente aus den letzten Jahren 1799–1800*,
> *Gesammelte Werke*, No. 3056, vol. IV, p. 302.)

WILLIAM WORDSWORTH

Aristotle, I have been told, has said that Poetry is the most philosophic of all writing: it is so: its object is truth, not individual and local, but general, and operative; not standing upon external testimony, but carried alive into the heart by passion; truth which is its own testimony, which gives competence and confidence to the tribunal to which it appeals, and receives them from the same tribunal. Poetry is the image of man and nature.

(*Preface to 'Lyrical Ballads', Poetical Works*, vol. II,
pp. 394–5.)

*   *   *   *   *

Poetry is the first and last of all knowledge – it is as immortal as the heart of man. If the labours of Men of science should ever create any material revolution, direct or indirect, in our condition, and in the impressions which we habitually receive, the Poet will sleep then no more than at present; he will be ready to follow the steps of the Man of science, not only in those general indirect effects, but he will be at his side, carrying sensation into the midst of the objects of the science itself. The remotest discoveries of the Chemist, the Botanist, or Mineralogist, will be as proper objects of the Poet's art as any upon which it can be employed, if the time should ever come when these things shall be familiar to us, and the relations under which they are contemplated by the followers of these respective sciences shall be manifestly and palpably material to us as enjoying and suffering beings. If the time should ever come when what is now called science, thus familiarised to men, shall be ready to put on, as it were, a form of flesh and blood, the Poet will lend his divine spirit to aid the transfiguration, and will welcome the Being thus produced, as a dear and genuine inmate of the household of man. – It is not, then, to be supposed that any one, who holds that sublime notion of Poetry which I have attempted to convey, will break in upon the sanctity and truth of his pictures by transitory and accidental ornaments, and endeavour to excite admiration of himself by arts, the necessity of which must manifestly depend upon the assumed meanness of his subject.

(Preface to 'Lyrical Ballads', Poetical Works, vol. II, pp. 396–7.)

*   *   *   *   *

The appropriate business of poetry, (which, nevertheless, if genuine, is as permanent as pure science,) her appropriate employment, her privilege and her *duty*, is to treat of things not as they *are*, but as they *appear*; not as they exist in themselves, but as they *seem* to exist to the *senses*, and to the *passions*.

(Preface to 'Lyrical Ballads', Poetical Works, vol. II, p. 410.)

*   *   *   *   *

The commerce between Man and his Maker cannot be carried on but by a process where much is represented in little, and the Infinite Being accommodates himself to a finite capacity. In all this may be perceived the affinity between religion and poetry; between religion – making up the deficiencies of reason by faith; and poetry – passionate for the instruction of reason; between religion – whose element is infinitude, and whose ultimate trust is the supreme of things, submitting herself to circumspection, and reconciled to substitutions; and poetry – ethereal and transcendent, yet incapable to sustain her existence without sensuous incarnation.

(Preface to 'Lyrical Ballads', Poetical Works, vol. II, p. 412.)

JOHN KEATS

In Poetry I have a few Axioms, and you will see how far I am from their Centre. 1st I think Poetry should surprise by a fine excess and not by Singularity – it should strike the Reader as a wording of his own highest thoughts, and appear almost a Remembrance – 2nd Its touches of Beauty should never be half way ther[e]by making the reader breathless instead of content: the rise, the progress, the setting of imagery should like the Sun come natural natural too him – shine over him and set soberly although in magnificence leaving him in the Luxury of twilight – but it is easier to think what Poetry should be than to write it – and this leads me on to another axiom. That if Poetry comes not as naturally as the Leaves to a tree it had better not come at all.

(Letter to John Taylor, 27 February 1818, *Letters*, p. 107.)

PERCY BYSSHE SHELLEY

Poetry is indeed something divine. It is at once the centre and circumference of knowledge; it is that which comprehends all science, and that to which all science must be referred. It is at the same time the root and blossom of all other systems of thought; it is that from which all spring, and that which adorns all; and that which, if blighted, denies the fruit and the seed, and withholds from the barren world the nourishment and the succession of the scions of the tree of life. It is the perfect and consummate surface and bloom of things; it is as the odour and the colour of the rose to the texture of the elements which compose it, as the form and the splendour of unfaded beauty to the secrets of anatomy and corruption. What were Virtue, Love, Patriotism, Friendship – what were the scenery of this beautiful Universe which we inhabit; what were our consolations on this side of the grave, and what were aspirations beyond it, if Poetry did not ascend to bring light and fire from those eternal regions where the owl-winged faculty of calculation dare not ever soar?

(A Defence of Poetry, Complete Works, vol. VII,
p. 135.)

* * * * *

All high poetry is infinite; it is as the first acorn, which contained all oaks potentially. Veil after veil may be undrawn, and the inmost naked beauty of the meaning never exposed. A great poem is a fountain for ever overflowing with the waters of wisdom and delight; and after one person and one age has exhausted all its divine effluence which their peculiar relations enable them to share, another and yet another succeeds, and new relations are ever developed, the source of an unforeseen and an unconceived delight.

(A Defence of Poetry, Complete Works, vol. VII,
p. 131.)

* * * * *

But Poetry acts in another and diviner manner. It awakens and enlarges the mind itself by rendering it the receptacle of a thousand unapprehended combinations of thought. Poetry lifts the veil from the hidden beauty of the world, and makes familiar objects be as if they were not familiar; it reproduces all that it represents, and the impersonations clothed in its Elysian light stand thenceforward in the minds of those who have once contemplated them, as memorials of that gentle and exalted content which extends itself over all thoughts and actions with which it coexists.

(A Defence of Poetry, Complete Works, vol. VII,
pp. 117–18.)

* * * * *

Poetry thus makes immortal all that is best and most beautiful in the world; it arrests the vanishing apparitions which haunt the interlunations of life, and veiling them, or in language or in form, sends them forth among mankind, bearing sweet news of kindred joy to those with whom their sisters abide – abide, because there is no portal of expression from the caverns of the spirit which they inhabit into the universe of things. Poetry redeems from decay the visitations of the divinity in Man.

Poetry turns all things to loveliness; it exalts the beauty of that which is most beautiful, and it adds beauty to that which is most deformed; it marries exultation and horror, grief and pleasure, eternity and change; it subdues to union under its light yoke, all irreconcilable things. It transmutes all that it touches, and every form moving within the radiance of its presence is changed by wondrous sympathy to an incarnation of the spirit which it breathes; its secret alchemy turns to potable gold the poisonous waters which flow from death through life; it strips the veil of familiarity from the world, and lays bare the naked and sleeping beauty, which is the spirit of its forms.

All things exist as they are perceived; at least in relation to the percipient. 'The mind is its own place, and of itself can make a Heaven of Hell, a Hell of Heaven.' But poetry defeats the curse which binds us to be subjected to the accident of surrounding impressions. And whether it spreads its own figured curtain, or withdraws life's dark veil from before the scene of things, it equally creates for us a being within our being. It makes us the inhabitants of a world to which the familiar world is a chaos. It reproduces the common Universe of which we are portions and percipients, and it purges from our inward sight the film of familiarity which obscures from us the wonder of our being. It compels us to feel that which we perceive, and to imagine that which we know. It creates anew the universe, after it has been annihilated in our minds by the recurrence of impressions blunted by reiteration. It justifies that bold and true word of Tasso: *Non merita nome di creatore, se non Iddio ed il Poeta.*

(*A Defence of Poetry, Complete Works*, vol. VII, pp. 137–8.)

VICTOR HUGO

Thus the aim of art is almost divine: to bring back to life, if it is making history; to create, if it is making poetry.

Ainsi le but de l'art est presque divin: ressusciter, s'il fait de l'histoire; créer, s'il fait de la poésie.

(*Préface de 'Cromwell'*, p. 91.)

ALPHONSE DE LAMARTINE

The world is young, for the mind still sees immense scope for progress between mankind's present state and the goal it can achieve; in that progress, poetry will have a new and high destiny to fulfil.

It will no longer be lyrical in our sense of the word; it has not enough youth, freshness or spontaneity to sing as it did at the dawn of human thought. It will no longer be epic; man has lived and meditated too long to be amused or interested by extensive epics, and experience has undermined his belief in the marvels with which the epic poem cast its spell. It will no longer be dramatic, because in our age of freedom and political action, the stage of real life has more urgent, more cogent and more personal import than the theatrical stage.

[. . .]

Poetry will be reason set to song, that is its destiny for long to come; it will be philosophical, religious, political, social, like the periods that mankind will go through; above all, it will be intimate, personal, meditative and serious, no longer a play of wit, a melodious caprice of flighty, superficial thought, but the deep, true and sincere echo of the mind's loftiest ideas and the soul's most mysterious impressions. It will be man himself, and no longer his image, man in all his truth. The prefigurations of this transformation of poetry have been apparent for more than a century; they are increasing in our times. Poetry has more and more rid itself of its artificial form, it has almost no other form than its own. As the world has become more spiritual, so too poetry. It no longer wants puppets or contrivances; for the first thing that the reader does is to push aside the puppets and contrivances and to seek only poetry in the poetic work, to seek also the poet's soul within his poetry.

But will it be dead because it is truer, more sincere, more genuine than ever before? Of course not; it will have more life, more intensity, more effectiveness than ever before!

[. . .]

Apart from this philosophical, rational and social destiny of the poetry of the future, it has a new destiny too: it must follow the tendencies of institutions and of the press; it must go among the people, and become a direct concern to them, like religion, reason and philosophy.

Le monde est jeune, car la pensée mesure encore une distance incommensurable entre l'état actuel de l'humanité et le but qu'elle peut atteindre; la poésie aura d'ici là de nouvelles, de hautes destinées à remplir.

Elle ne sera plus lyrique dans le sens où nous prenons ce mot; elle n'a plus assez de jeunesse, de fraîcheur, de spontanéité d'impression, pour chanter comme au premier réveil de la pensée humaine. Elle ne sera plus épique; l'homme a trop vécu, trop réfléchi pour se laisser amuser, intéresser par les longs écrits de l'épopée, et l'expérience a détruit sa foi aux merveilles dont le poëme épique enchantait sa crédulité. Elle ne sera plus dramatique, parce que la scène de la vie réelle a, dans nos temps de liberté et d'action politique, un intérêt plus pressant, plus réel et plus intime que la scène du théâtre.

[. . .]

La poésie sera de la raison chantée, voilà sa destinée pour longtemps; elle sera philosophique, religieuse, politique, sociale, comme les époques que le genre humain va traverser; elle sera intime surtout, personnelle, méditative et grave; non plus un jeu de l'esprit, un caprice mélodieux de la pensée légère et superficielle, mais l'écho profond, réel, sincère, des plus hautes conceptions de l'intelligence, des plus mystérieuses impressions de l'âme. Ce sera l'homme lui-même et non plus son image, l'homme sincère et tout entier. Les signes avant-coureurs de cette transformation de la poésie sont visibles depuis plus d'un siècle; ils se multiplient de nos jours. La poésie s'est dépouillée de plus en plus de sa forme artificielle, elle n'a presque plus de forme qu'elle-même. A mesure que tout s'est spiritualisé dans le monde, elle aussi se spiritualise. Elle ne veut plus de mannequin, elle n'invente plus de machine; car la première chose que fait maintenant l'esprit du lecteur, c'est de dépouiller le mannequin, c'est de démonter la machine et de chercher la poésie seule dans l'œuvre poétique, et de chercher aussi l'âme du poëte sous sa poésie.

Mais sera-t-elle morte pour être plus vraie, plus sincère, plus réelle qu'elle ne le fut jamais? Non sans doute; elle aura plus de vie, plus d'intensité, plus d'action qu'elle n'en eut encore!

[. . .]

A côté de cette destinée philosophique, rationnelle, politique, sociale de la poésie à venir, elle a une destinée nouvelle à accomplir: elle doit suivre la pente des institutions et de la presse; elle doit se faire peuple, et devenir populaire comme la religion, la raison et la philosophie.

(*Des Destinées de la Poésie*, *Œuvres complètes*, vol. I, pp. 57–60.)

THE ROLE OF THE POET

NOVALIS

We are engaged on a mission: we are called to give shape to the earth.

Wir sind auf einer Mission: zur Bildung der Erde sind wir berufen.

> (*Blütenstaub*, No. 32, *Gesammelte Werke*, vol. II, p. 17.)

*   *   *   *   *

Poets and priests were in the beginning *one*, and only later ages have separated them. But the true poet has always remained a priest, just as the true priest has always remained a poet. And should not the future restore the old state of affairs?

Dichter und Priester waren im Anfang *eins*, und nur spätere Zeiten haben sie getrennt. Der echte Dichter ist aber immer Priester, so wie der echte Priester immer Dichter geblieben. Und sollte nicht die Zukunft den alten Zustand der Dinge wieder herbeiführen?

> (*Blütenstaub*, No. 71, *Gesammelte Werke*, vol. II, p. 25.)

*   *   *   *   *

The artist stands above the human being, like the statue on its pedestal.

Der Künstler steht auf dem Menschen, wie die Statue auf dem Piedestal.

> (*Fragmente des Jahres 1798, Gesammelte Werke*, No. 814, vol. III, p. 24.)

*   *   *   *   *

The artist is wholly transcendental.

Der Künstler ist durchaus transzendental.

> (*Fragmente des Jahres 1798, Gesammelte Werke*, No. 816, vol. III, p. 25.)

*   *   *   *   *

Only an artist can divine the meaning of life.

Nur ein Künstler kann den Sinn des Lebens erraten.

> (*Fragmente des Jahres 1798, Gesammelte Werke*, No. 951, vol. III, p. 60.)

FRIEDRICH SCHLEGEL

Only he who has a religion of his own, an original view of the infinite, can be an artist.

Nur derjenige kann ein Künstler sein, welcher eine eigne Religion, eine originelle Ansicht des Unendlichen hat.

> (*Ideen*, No. 13, *Kritische Ausgabe*, vol. II, p. 257.)

*   *   *   *   *

As mankind is to the other creations on earth, so artists are to mankind.

Was die Menschen unter den andern Bildungen der Erde, das sind die Künstler unter den Menschen.

(*Athenäum Fragment*, No. 43, *Kritische Ausgabe*, vol. II, p. 260.)

*   *   *   *   *

We cannot see God, but we can see the divine everywhere, most immediately and truly, however, at the core of an understanding human being, in the depths of a living human work. You can feel and think nature and the universe directly, but not the divinity. Only the human being among human beings can create and think in a divine way, and live with religion. No one can be a direct mediator unto himself for his own spirit, because the mediator must be simply object, whose centre the contemplator posits outside himself. One chooses and posits one's mediator, but one can only choose and posit him who has already posited himself as such. A mediator is he who perceives the divine in himself, and who self-destructively surrenders his self in order to proclaim and communicate this divine perception, and to present it to all mankind in ethos and action, in words and works. If this urge does not follow, then what was perceived was not divine or not personal. To mediate and to receive meditation is mankind's whole higher life, and every artist is a mediator for all others.

Gott erblicken wir nicht, aber überall erblicken wir Göttliches; zunächst und am eigentlichsten jedoch in der Mitte eines sinnvollen Menschen, in der Tiefe eines lebendigen Menschenwerks. Die Natur, das Universum kannst du unmittelbar fühlen, unmittelbar denken; nicht also die Gottheit. Nur der Mensch unter Menschen kann göttlich dichten und denken und mit Religion leben. Sich selbst kann niemand auch nur seinem Geiste direkter Mittler sein, weil dieser schlechthin Objekt sein muss, dessen Zentrum der Anschauende ausser sich setzt. Man

wählt und setzt sich den Mittler, aber man kann sich nur den
wählen und setzen, der sich schon als solchen gesetzt hat. Ein
Mittler ist derjenige, der Göttliches in sich wahrnimmt, und
sich selbst vernichtend preisgibt, um dieses Göttliche zu ver-
kündigen, mitzuteilen, und darzustellen allen Menschen in Sit-
ten und Taten, in Worten und Werken. Erfolgt dieser Trieb
nicht, so war das Wahrgenommene nicht göttlich oder nicht
eigen. Vermitteln und Vermitteltwerden ist das ganze höhere
Leben des Menschen, und jeder Künstler ist Mittler für alle
übrigen.

(*Athenäum Fragment*, No. 44, *Kritische Ausgabe*, vol.
II, p. 260.)

*   *   *   *   *

Through artists mankind becomes an individual in that they
link past and future in the present. They are the higher organs of
the soul, the point where the vital external forces of mankind
converge, and where the inner forces are in most immediate
effect.

Durch die Künstler wird die Menschheit ein Individuum,
indem sie Vorwelt und Nachwelt in der Gegenwart verknüpfen.
Sie sind das höhere Seelenorgan, wo die Lebensgeister der
ganzen äussern Menschheit zusammentreffen und in welchem
die innere zunächst wirkt.

(*Athenäum Fragment*, No. 64, *Kritische Ausgabe*, vol.
II, p. 262.)

*   *   *   *   *

Even in outer habits the artists' way of life should be clearly
distinct from that of the majority. They are the Brahmins, a
higher caste, ennobled not by birth but by voluntary self-
dedication.

1798-1800

Selbst in den äusserlichen Gebräuchen sollte sich die Lebensart der Künstler von der Lebensart der übrigen Menschen
durchaus unterscheiden. Sie sind Brahminen, eine höhere
Kaste, aber nicht durch Geburt sondern durch freie Selbstein-
weihung geadelt.

(*Athenäum Fragment*, No. 146, *Kritische Ausgabe*,
vol. II, p. 271.)

WILLIAM WORDSWORTH

Taking up the subject, then, upon general grounds, let me
ask, what is meant by the word Poet? What is a Poet? To whom
does he address himself? And what language is to be expected
from him? – He is a man speaking to men: a man, it is true,
endowed with more lively sensibility, more enthusiasm and
tenderness, who has a greater knowledge of human nature, and
a more comprehensive soul, than are supposed to be common
among mankind; a man pleased with his own passions and
volitions, and who rejoices more than other men in the spirit of
life that is in him; delighting to contemplate similar volitions
and passions as manifested in the goings-on of the Universe, and
habitually impelled to create them where he does not find them.
To these qualities he has added a disposition to be affected more
than other men by absent things as if they were present; an
ability of conjuring up in himself passions, which are indeed far
from being the same as those produced by real events, yet
(especially in those parts of the general sympathy which are
pleasing and delightful) do more nearly resemble the passions produced by real events, then anything which, from the
motions of their own minds merely, other men are accustomed to feel in themselves: – whence, and from practice,
he has acquired a greater readiness and power in expressing
what he thinks and feels, and especially those thoughts and
feelings which, by his own choice, or from the structure

of his own mind, arise in him without immediate external excitement.

(*Preface to 'Lyrical Ballads', Poetical Works*, vol. II, p. 393.)

*　　*　　*　　*　　*

To this knowledge which all men carry about with them, and to these sympathies in which, without any other discipline than that of our daily life, we are fitted to take delight, the Poet principally directs his attention. He considers man and nature as essentially adapted to each other, and the mind of man as naturally the mirror of the fairest and most interesting properties of nature. And thus the Poet, prompted by this feeling of pleasure, which accompanies him through the whole course of his studies, converses with general nature, with affections akin to those, which, through labour and length of time, the Man of science has raised up in himself, by conversing with those particular parts of nature which are the objects of his studies. The knowledge both of the Poet and the Man of science is pleasure; but the knowledge of the one cleaves to us as a necessary part of our existence, our natural and unalienable inheritance; the other is a personal and individual acquisition, slow to come to us, and by no habitual and direct sympathy connecting us with our fellow-beings. The Man of science seeks truth as a remote and unknown benefactor; he cherishes and loves it in his solitude: the Poet, singing a song in which all human beings join with him, rejoices in the presence of truth as our visible friend and hourly companion. Poetry is the breath and finer spirit of all knowledge; it is the impassioned expression which is in the countenance of all Science. Emphatically may it be said of the Poet, as Shakspeare hath said of man, 'that he looks before and after'. He is the rock of defence for human nature; an upholder and preserver, carrying everywhere with him relationship and love. In spite of difference of soil and climate, of language and

manners, of laws and customs: in spite of things silently gone
out of mind, and things violently destroyed; the Poet binds
together by passion and knowledge the vast empire of human
society, as it spread over the whole earth, and over all time.

(Preface to 'Lyrical Ballads', Poetical Works, vol. II,
p. 296.)

SAMUEL TAYLOR COLERIDGE

Sensibility indeed, both quick and deep, is not only a characteristic feature, but may be deemed a component part, of
genius. But it is not less an essential mark of true genius, that its
sensibility is excited by any other cause more powerfully than by
its own personal interests; for this plain reason, that the man of
genius lives most in the ideal world, in which the present is still
constituted by the future or the past; and because his feelings
have been habitually associated with thoughts and images, to
the number, clearness, and vivacity of which the sensation of *self*
is always in an inverse proportion.

(Biographia Literaria, chapter 2, vol. I, p. 30.)

*   *   *   *   *

My own conclusions on the nature of poetry, in the strictest
use of the word, have been in part anticipated in the preceding
disquisition on the fancy and imagination. What is poetry? is so
nearly the same question with, what is a poet? that the answer to
the one is involved in the solution of the other. For it is a
distinction resulting from the poetic genius itself, which sus-
tains and modifies the images, thoughts, and emotions of the
poet's own mind.

The poet, described in *ideal* perfection, brings the whole soul
of man into activity, with the subordination of its faculties to
each other, according to their relative worth and dignity. He

diffuses a tone and spirit of unity, that blends, and (as it were) *fuses*, each into each, by that synthetic and magical power, to which we have exclusively appropriated the name of imagination. This power, first put in action by the will and understanding, and retained under their irremissive, though gentle and unnoticed, control (*laxis effertur habenis*) reveals itself in the balance or reconciliation of opposite or discordant qualities: of sameness, with difference; of the general, with the concrete; the idea, with the image; the individual, with the representative; the sense of novelty and freshness, with old and familiar objects; a more than usual state of emotion, with more than usual order; judgement ever awake and steady self-possession, with enthusiasm and feeling profound or vehement; and while it blends and harmonizes the natural and the artificial, still subordinates art to nature; the manner to the matter; and our admiration of the poet to our sympthathy with the poetry. 'Doubtless,' as Sir John Davies observes of the soul (and his words may with slight alteration be applied, and even more appropriately, to the poetic IMAGINATION)

'Doubtless this could not be, but that she turns
    Bodies to spirit by sublimation strange,
As fire converts to fire the things it burns,
    As we our food into our nature change.

From their gross matter she abstracts their forms,
    And draws a kind of quintessence from things;
Which to her proper nature she transforms,
    To bear them light on her celestial wings.

Thus does she, when from individual states
    She doth abstract the universal kinds;
Which then re-clothed in divers names and fates
    Steal access through our senses to our minds.'

Finally, GOOD SENSE is the BODY of poetic genius, FANCY its DRAPERY, MOTION its LIFE, and IMAGINATION the

SOUL that is everywhere, and in each; and forms all into one
graceful and intelligent whole.

> (*Biographia Literaria*, chapter 14, vol. II,
> pp. 12–13.)

VICTOR HUGO

What, after all, is a poet? A man who has strong feelings and
who puts them into expressive language. Poetry is almost
nothing other than feeling.

Qu'est-ce, en effet, qu'un poète? Un homme qui sent forte-
ment, exprimant ses sensations dans une langue expressive. La
poésie, ce n'est presque que sentiment.

> ('Sur André Chénier' (1819), *Œuvres complètes*, vol.
> XVII, p. 130.)

PERCY BYSSHE SHELLEY

. . . to be a poet is to apprehend the true and the beautiful, in a
word, the good which exists in the relation, subsisting, first
between existence and perception, and secondly between perception and expression. . . .

But poets, or those who imagine and express this indestructible order, are not only the authors of language and of music, or
the dance and architecture, and statuary, and painting; they are
the institutors of laws, and the founders of civil society, and the
inventors of the arts of life, and the teachers, who draw into a
certain propinquity with the beautiful and the true, that partial
apprehension of the agencies of the invisible world which is
called religion. Hence all original religions are allegorical, or
susceptible of allegory, and, like Janus, have a double face of
false and true. Poets, according to the circumstances of the age
and nation in which they appeared, were called, in the earlier

epochs of the world, legislators, or prophets: a poet essentially comprises and unites both these characters. For he not only beholds intensely the present as it is, and discovers those laws according to which present things ought to be ordered, but he beholds the future in the present, and his thoughts are the germs of the flower and the fruit of latest time. Not that I assert poets to be prophets in the gross sense of the word, or that they can foretell the form as surely as they foreknow the spirit of events: such is the pretence of superstition, which would make poetry an attribute of prophecy, rather than prophecy an attribute of poetry. A poet participates in the eternal, the infinite, and the one; as far as relates to his conceptions, time and place and number are not.

(*A Defence of Poetry, Complete Works*, vol. VII, pp. 111–12.)

* * * * *

Poets are the hierophants of an unapprehended inspiration; the mirrors of the gigantic shadows which futurity casts upon the present; the words which express what they understand not; the trumpets which sing to battle, and feel not what they inspire; the influence which is moved not, but moves. Poets are the unacknowledged legislators of the world.

(*A Defence of Poetry, Complete Works*, vol. VII, p. 140.)

PIERRE-SIMON BALLANCHE

The poet simply translates into human language what has been revealed to him on the spiritual level.

[. . .]

It is always a religious truth that the poet has to transmit. Religion and poetry are but one and the same. The poet is a priest.

Le poète ne fait que traduire en paroles humaines ce que lui a été révélé sur le plan spirituel.

[. . .]

C'est toujours une vérité religieuse que le poète est chargé de transmettre. Religion et poésie ne font qu'une seule et même chose. Le poète est prêtre.

(*Orphée*, *Œuvres complètes*, vol. VI, pp. 82 and 96.)

ALFRED DE VIGNY

I heard Chatterton's deep, gentle voice making this strange reply, jerking the words out, and halting at each phrase:

'England is a ship: our island is that shape; her prow turned to the North, she is, as it were, at anchor in mid-sea, keeping watch over the continent. She continually produces other ships made in her own image, who go to represent her on all the coasts of the world. But it is on board the great ship that the work of everyone of us takes place. The king, the lords, the commons are at the flag, the helm, the compass; the rest of us must all man the ropes, climb the masts, unfurl the sails and load the canons; we are all part of the crew, and no one is without his use in the handling of our glorious ship.'

This created a sensation. They drew nearer without really understanding and without knowing whether they should jeer or applaud, as so often happens to ordinary people.

– *Well! very well!* shouted big Beckford. That's fine, my child! Our fortunate country is nobly represented! *Rule Britannia!* he sang, humming the national song. But, my boy, I take you at your word. What the devil can the poet do in the handling of this ship?

Chatterton kept his initial calm; it was the calm of a man absorbed in an incessant inner process that makes him feel shadowed by phantoms. He only raised his eyes to the ceiling, and said:

– The poet seeks out in the stars which route God's finger indicates to us.

J'entendis la voix creuse et douce de Chatterton, qui fit cette singulière réponse en saccadant ses paroles, et s'arrêtant à chaque phrase:

'L'Angleterre est un vaisseau: notre île en a la forme; la proue tournée au nord, elle est comme à l'ancre au milieu des mers, surveillant le continent. Sans cesse elle tire de ses flancs d'autres vaisseaux faits à son image et qui vont la représenter sur toutes les côtes du monde. Mais c'est à bord du grand navire qu'est notre ouvrage à tous. Le roi, les lords, les communes sont au pavillon, au gouvernail et à la boussole; nous autres, nous devons tous avoir la main aux cordages, monter aux mâts, tendre les voiles et charger les canons: nous sommes tous de l'équipage, et nul n'est inutile dans la manoeuvre de notre glorieux navire.'

Cela fit sensation. On s'approcha sans trop comprendre et sans savoir si l'on devait se moquer ou applaudir, situation accoutumée du vulgaire.

– *Well! very well!* cria le gros Beckford; c'est bien, mon enfant! c'est noblement représenter notre bienheureuse patrie! *Rule Britannia!* chanta-t-il en fredonnant l'air national. Mais, mon garçon, je vous prends par vos paroles. Que diable peut faire le poète dans la manoeuvre?

Chatterton resta dans sa première immobilité; c'était celle d'un homme absorbé par un travail intérieur qui ne cesse jamais et qui lui fait voir des ombres sur ses pas. Il leva seulement les yeux au plafond, et dit:

– Le poète cherche aux étoiles quelle route nous montre le doigt du Seigneur.

(*Stello*, chapter XVII, *Œuvres complètes*, vol. I, pp. 626–7.)

THE CREATIVE IMAGINATION

WILLIAM BLAKE

And I know that This World Is a World of imagination & Vision. I see Every thing I paint in This World, but Every body does not see alike. To the Eyes of a Miser a Guinea is more beautiful than the Sun, & a bag worn with the use of Money has more beautiful proportions than a Vine filled with Grapes. The tree which moves some to tears of joy is in the Eyes of others only a Green thing that stands in the way. Some See Nature all Ridicule & Deformity, & by these I shall not regulate my proportions; & Some Scarce see Nature at all. But to the Eyes of the Man of Imagination, Nature is Imagination itself. As a man is, So he Sees. As the Eye is formed, such are its Powers. You certainly Mistake, when you say that the Visions of Fancy are not to be found in This World. To Me This World is all One continued Vision of Fancy or Imagination, & I feel Flatter'd when I am told so. What is it sets Homer, Virgil & Milton in so high a rank of Art? Why is the Bible more Entertaining & Instructive than any other book? Is it not because they are addressed to the Imagination, which is Spiritual Sensation, & but mediately to the Understanding or Reason? Such is True Painting, and such was alone valued by the Greeks & the best modern Artists.

(Letter to Dr Trusler, 23 August 1799, *Complete Writings*, pp. 793–4.)

*   *   *   *   *

This world of Imagination is the world of Eternity; it is the divine bosom into which we shall go after the death of the Vegetated body. This World of Imagination is Infinite & Eternal, whereas the world of Generation, or Vegetation, is Finite & Temporal. There Exist in that Eternal World the Permanent

Realities of Every Thing which we see reflected in this Vegetable Glass of Nature.

(*A Vision of the Last Judgement*, *Complete Writings*, p. 605.)

* * * * *

I assert for My Self that I do not behold the outward Creation & that to me it is hindrance & not Action; it is as the Dirt upon my feet, No part of Me. 'What,' it will be Question'd, 'When the Sun rises, do you not see a round disk of fire somewhat like a Guinea?' O no, no, I see an Innumerable company of the Heavenly host crying "Holy, Holy, Holy is the Lord God Almighty." I question not my Corporeal or Vegetative Eye any more than I would Question a Window concerning a Sight. I look thro' it & not with it.

(*A Vision of the Last Judgement*, *Complete Writings*, p. 617.)

NOVALIS

The imagination puts the future world either up in the heights, or down in the depths, or in some transubstantiation. We dream of journeys through the universe: is the universe not within us? We do not know the depths of our souls. It is inwards that the mysterious path leads. Within us, or nowhere lies eternity and its worlds, the past and the future. The outer world is a world of shadows, it casts its shadows onto the realm of light.

Die Phantasie setzt die künftige Welt entweder in die Höhe, oder in die Tiefe, oder in der Metempsychose zu uns. Wir träumen von Reisen durch das Weltall: ist denn das Weltall nicht in uns? Die Tiefen unsers Geistes kennen wir nicht. – Nach Innen geht der geheimnisvolle Weg. In uns, oder nirgends ist die Ewigkeit mit ihren Welten, die Vergangenheit und die Zukunft. Die Aussenwelt ist die Schattenwelt, sie wirft ihren Schatten in das Lichtreich.

(*Blütenstaub*, No. 16, *Gesammelte Werke*, vol. II, p. 13.)

*   *   *   *   *

To make poetry is to create. All poetry must be living and individual. What an inexhaustible mass of materials is at hand for *new* individual combinations! He who has grasped this secret, needs only to decide to renounce the mere enjoyment of the endless multiplicity and to *make a start* somewhere – but this decision is at the expense of the free consciousness of our infinite world and demands limitation to a single aspect.

Perhaps we should ascribe our earthly existence to such a decision?

Dichten ist Zeugen. Alles Gedichtete muss ein lebendiges Individuum sein. Welche unerschöpfliche Menge von Materialien zu *neuen* individuellen Kombinationen liegt nicht umher! Wer einmal dieses Geheimnis erraten hat, der hat nichts mehr nötig als den Entschluss, der unendlichen Mannigfaltigkeit und ihrem blossen Genusse zu entsagen und irgendwo *anzufangen* – aber dieser Entschluss kostet das freie Gefühl einer unendlichen Welt und fordert die Beschränkung auf eine einzelne Erscheinung derselben.

Sollten wir vielleicht einem ähnlichen Entschlusse unser irdisches Dasein zuzuschreiben haben?

(*Fragmente des Jahres 1798*, *Gesammelte Werke*, No. 812, vol. III, p. 24.)

FRIEDRICH SCHLEGEL

. . . it is the holy breath that touches us in the sound of music. It cannot be grasped forcibly and captured mechanically, but it can be gently wooed by mortal beauty and enfolded in it; and the magic words of poetry can also be charged and inspired by its power. But in any poem, where it is, or could not be, everywhere present, it is certainly not present at all. It is an infinite being, and assuredly does not adhere or attach its interest only to persons, events, situations and individual inclinations: for the true poet, all this, however close to his soul, is merely a pointer to the higher, the infinite, a hieroglyph of the One eternal love and of the holy living fullness of creative nature.

Imagination alone can grasp the mystery of love and present it as a mystery; and this mysterious quality is the source of all that is imaginative in the form of poetic representation. Imagination strives with all its might to express itself, but the divine can be conveyed and expressed only indirectly in the sphere of nature. For this reason, all that remains in the world of appearances of what was originally imagination is that which we call wit.

. . . es ist der heilige Hauch, der uns in den Tönen der Musik berührt. Er lässt sich nicht gewaltsam fassen und mechanisch greifen, aber er lässt sich freundlich locken von sterblicher Schönheit und in sie verhüllen; und auch die Zauberworte der Poesie können von seiner Kraft durchdrungen und beseelt werden. Aber in dem Gedicht, wo er nicht überall ist, oder überall sein könnte, ist er gewiss gar nicht. Er ist ein unendliches Wesen und mitnichten haftet und klebt sein Interesse nur an den Personen, den Begebenheiten und Situationen und den individuellen Neigungen: für den wahren Dichter ist alles dieses, so innig es auch seine Seele umschliessen mag, nur Hindeutung auf das Höhere, Unendliche, Hieroglyphe der Einen ewigen Liebe und der heiligen Lebensfülle der bildenden Natur.

Nur die Fantasie kann das Rätsel dieser Liebe fassen und als Rätsel darstellen; und dieses Rätselhafte ist die Quelle von dem Fantastischen in der Form aller poetischen Darstellung. Die Fantasie strebt aus allen Kräften sich zu äussern, aber das Göttliche kann sich in der Sphäre der Natur nur indirekt mitteilen und äussern. Daher bleibt von dem, was ursprünglich Fantasie war, in der Welt der Erscheinungen nur das zurück was wir Witz nennen.

(*Gespräch über die Poesie*, *Kritische Werke*, vol. II, p. 334.)

WILLIAM WORDSWORTH

Imagination, in the sense of the word as giving title to a class of the following Poems, has no reference to images that are merely a faithful copy, existing in the mind, of absent external objects; but is a word of higher import, denoting operations of the mind upon those objects, and processes of creation or of composition, governed by certain fixed laws.

(*Preface to 'Lyrical Ballads'*, *Poetical Works*, vol. II, p. 436.)

*   *   *   *   *

When the Imagination frames a comparison, if it does not strike on the first presentation, a sense of the truth of the likeness, from the moment that it is perceived, grows – and continues to grow – upon the mind; the resemblance depending less upon outline of form and feature, than upon expression and effect; less upon casual and outstanding, than upon inherent and internal, properties: moreover, the images invariably modify each other. – The law under which the processes of Fancy are carried on is as capricious as the accidents of things, and the effects are surprising, playful, ludicrous, amusing, tender, or pathetic, as the objects happen to be appositely produced or fortunately combined. Fancy depends upon the rapidity and profusion with which she scatters her thoughts and images; trusting that their number, and the felicity with which they are linked together, will make amends for the want of individual value: or she prides herself upon the curious subtilty and the successful elaboration with which she can detect their lurking affinities. If she can win you over to her purpose, and impart to you her feelings, she cares not how unstable or transitory may be her influence, knowing that it will not be out of her power to resume it upon an apt occasion. But the Imagination is conscious of an indestructible dominion; – the Soul may fall away from it, not being able to sustain its grandeur; but, if once felt and acknowledged, by no act of any other faculty of the mind can it be relaxed, impaired, or diminished. – Fancy is given to quicken and to beguile the temporal part of our nature, Imagination to incite and to support the eternal.

(*Preface to 'Lyrical Ballads', Poetical Works*, vol. II,
pp. 441–2.)

AUGUST WILHELM SCHLEGEL

The dead and empirical view of the world is that things are; the philosophical view is that everything is in an eternal process of becoming, an incessant creation, as is shown by a host of phenomena in common life. From time immemorial man has subsumed this active, generative force into a single concept, namely that of nature in its truest and highest sense. In no single thing produced can this universal creative force be extinguished, but we can never perceive it with our outer senses, we can recognise it most distinctly at that point where we ourselves bear our share of it, as organic beings and according to the extent of our relationship to other structures. The whole of nature is likewise structured, but we cannot see that; nature is an intelligence, like us; we can merely intuit this, and achieve a clear insight only through speculation. If nature is taken in this loftiest sense, not as a mass of generated objects, but as the generator itself; and if, moreover, the term imitation is also taken in its nobler meaning, whereby it does not connote an aping of man's externals, but an adoption of the maxims governing his actions, then there is neither further objection nor addition to the thesis: art should imitate nature. That is to say: like nature, it should create independently, structured and structuring, shape living works, which move not through an extraneous mechanism, like a pendulum clock, but through an innate force, like the solar system, and which return to their own self-contained perfection.

Die tote und empirische Ansicht von der Welt ist, dass die Dinge sind, die philosophische, dass alles im ewigen Werden, in einer unaufhörlichen Schöpfung begriffen ist, worauf uns schon eine Menge Erscheinungen im gemeinen Leben gleichsam hinstossen. Von uralten Zeiten her hat daher auch der Mensch diese in allem wirksame Kraft der Hervorbringung zur Einheit einer Idee zusammengefasst, und das ist die Natur im eigentlichsten und höchsten Sinne. In keinem einzelnen Produkte kann diese universelle Schöpferkraft erlöschen, allein wir können sie nie mit dem äusseren Sinne gewahrwerden; am bestimmtesten erkennen wir sie von dem Punkte aus, wo wir selbst unseren Anteil daran in uns tragen, als organische Wesen und nach den Graden der Verwandtschaft anderer Organisationen mit der unsrigen. Die gesamte Natur ist ebenfalls organisiert, aber das sehen wir nicht; sie ist eine Intelligenz wie wir, das ahnen wir nun und gelangen erst durch Spekulation zur klaren Einsicht. Wird nun Natur in dieser würdigsten Bedeutung genommen, nicht als eine Masse von Produkten, sondern als das Produzierende selbst, und der Ausdruck Nachahmung ebenfalls in dem edleren Sinne, wo es nicht heisst, die Äusserlichkeiten eines Menschen nachäffen, sondern sich die Maximen seines Handelns zu eigen machen, so ist nichts mehr gegen den Grundsatz einzuwenden, noch zu ihm hinzuzufügen: die Kunst soll die Natur nachahmen. Das heisst nämlich, sie soll wie die Natur selbständig schaffend, organisiert und organisierend, lebendige Werke bilden, die nicht erst durch einen fremden Mechanismus, wie etwa eine Pendeluhr, sondern durch inwohnende Kraft, wie das Sonnensystem, beweglich sind, und vollendet in sich selbst zurückkehren.

(*Vorlesungen über schöne Kunst und Literatur*, *Kritische Schriften*, vol. II, pp. 90–1.)

JOHN KEATS

O I wish I was as certain of the end of all your troubles as that of your momentary start about the authenticity of the Imagination. I am certain of nothing but of the holiness of the Heart's affections and the truth of Imagination – What the imagination seizes as Beauty must be truth – whether it existed before or not – for I have the same Idea of all our Passions as of Love they are all in their sublime, creative of essential Beauty – In a Word, you may know my favourite Speculation by my first Book and the little song I sent in my last – which is a representation from the fancy of the probable mode of operating in these Matters – The Imagination may be compared to Adam's dream – he awoke and found it truth. I am the more zealous in this affair, because I have never yet been able to perceive how any thing can be known for truth by consequitive reasoning – and yet it must be – Can it be that even the greatest Philosopher ever (when) arrived at his goal without putting aside numerous objections – However it may be, O for a Life of Sensations rather than of Thoughts! It is 'a Vision in the form of Youth' a Shadow of reality to come – and this consideration has further conv[i]nced me for it has come as auxiliary to another favourite Speculation of mine, that we shall enjoy ourselves here after by having what we

called happiness on Earth repeated in a finer tone and so repeated – And yet such a fate can only befall those who delight in
sensation rather than hunger as you do after Truth – Adam's
dream will do here and seems to be a conviction that Imagination and its empyreal reflection is the same as human Life and its
spiritual repetition. But as I was saying – the simple imaginative
Mind may have its rewards in the repeti[ti]on of its own silent
Working coming continually on the spirit with a fine sudden-
ness – to compare great things with small – have you never by
being surprised with an old Melody – in a delicious place – by a
delicious voice, fe[l]t over again your very speculations and
surmises at the time it first operated on your soul – do you not
remember forming to yourself the singer's face more beautiful
that [than] it was possible and yet with the elevation of the
Moment you did not think so – even then you were mounted on
the Wings of Imagination so high – that the Prototype must be
here after – that delicious face you will see – What a time!

(Letter to Benjamin Bailey, 22 November 1817,
Letters, pp. 67–8.)

SAMUEL TAYLOR COLERIDGE

"*Esemplastic. The word is not in Johnson, nor have I met with it
elsewhere.*" Neither have I. I constructed it myself from the
Greek words, εἰς ἕν πλάττειν, to shape into one; because, having
to convey a new sense, I thought that a new term would both aid
the recollection of my meaning, and prevent its being con-
founded with the usual import of the word, imagination.

(*Biographia Literaria*, chapter 10, vol. 1, p. 107.)

*   *   *   *   *

The IMAGINATION then, I consider either as primary, or
secondary. The primary IMAGINATION I hold to be the living

Power and prime Agent of all human Perception, and as a repetition in the finite mind of the eternal act of creation in the infinite I AM. The secondary Imagination I consider as an echo of the former, co-existing with the conscious will, yet still as identical with the primary in the *kind* of its agency, and differing only in *degree*, and in the *mode* of its operation. It dissolves, diffuses, dissipates, in order to recreate; or where this process is rendered impossible, yet still at all events it struggles to idealise and to unify. It is essentially *vital*, even as all objects (*as* objects) are essentially fixed and dead.

FANCY, on the contrary, has no other counters to play with, but fixities and definites. The Fancy is indeed no other than a mode of Memory emancipated from the order of time and space; while it is blended with, and modified by that empirical phenomenon of the will, which we express by the word CHOICE. But equally with the ordinary memory the Fancy must receive all its materials ready made from the law of association.

(*Biographia Literaria*, chapter 13, vol. I, p. 202.)

*   *   *   *   *

The poet should paint to the imagination, not to the fancy; and I know no happier case to exemplify the distinction between these two faculties. Master-pieces of the former mode of poetic painting abound in the writings of Milton, ex. gr.

> 'The fig-tree; not that kind for fruit renown'd,
> But such as at this day, to Indians known,
> In Malabar or Decan spreads her arms
> Branching so broad and long, that in the ground
> The bended twigs take root, *and daughters grow*
> *About the mother tree, a pillar'd shade*
> *High over-arch'd, and* ECHOING WALKS BETWEEN:
> *There oft the Indian Herdsman, shunning heat,*
> *Shelters in cool, and tends his pasturing herds*

At loop holes cut through thickest shade.'
MILTON P. L. 9. 1100.

This is *creation* rather than *painting*, or if painting, yet such, and with such co-presence of the whole picture flash'd at once upon the eye, as the sun paints in a camera obscura. But the poet must likewise understand and command what Bacon calls the *vestigia communia* of the senses, the latency of all in each, and more especially as by a magical *penna duplex*, the excitement of vision by sound and the exponents of sound. Thus "THE ECHOING WALKS BETWEEN", may be almost said to reverse the fable in tradition of the head of Memnon, in the Egyptian statue. Such may be deservedly entitled the *creative words* in the world of imagination.

(Biographia Literaria, chapter 22, vol. II,
pp. 102–3.)

PERCY BYSSHE SHELLEY

Poetry is not like reasoning, a power to be exerted according to the determination of the will. A man cannot say, 'I will compose poetry.' The greatest poet even cannot say it: for the mind in creation is as a fading coal, which some invisible influence, like an inconstant wind, awakens to transitory brightness: this power arises from within, like the colour of a flower which fades and changes as it is developed, and the conscious portions of our natures are unprophetic either of its approach or its departure. Could this influence be durable in its original purity and force, it is impossible to predict the greatness of the results; but when composition begins, inspiration is already on the decline, and the most glorious poetry that has ever been communicated to the world is probably a feeble shadow of the original conception of the Poet.

(A Defence of Poetry, Complete Works, vol. VII,
p. 135.)

VICTOR HUGO

The realm of poetry is without bound. Beneath the real world there is an ideal world which reveals itself in all its brilliance to the eye of those accustomed by serious meditation to see in things more than just things. The beautiful works of poetry of every kind, in verse or prose, that have brought glory to our century, have disclosed this heretofore hardly known truth, that poetry lies not in the form of the ideas, but in the ideas themselves. Poetry is the intimate essence of all that is.

Le domaine de la poésie est illimité. Sous le monde réel, il existe un monde idéal qui se montre resplendissant à l'œil de ceux que des méditations graves ont accoutumés à voir dans les choses plus que les choses. Les beaux ouvrages de poésie en tout genre, soit en vers, soit en prose, qui ont honoré notre siècle, ont révélé cette vérité à peine soupçonnée auparavant, que la poésie n'est pas dans la forme des idées, mais dans les idées elles-mêmes. La poésie, c'est tout ce qu'il y a d'intime dans tout.

(1822 Preface to *Odes*, *Œuvres poétiques*, vol. I, p. 265.)

THE SHAPES OF BEAUTY

FRIEDRICH SCHLEGEL

That is beautiful that reminds us of nature, and so stimulates the awareness of the infinite fullness of life. Nature is organic, and the highest beauty is therefore eternally vegetative, and the same holds true of morality and love.

Schön ist was uns an die Natur erinnert, und also das Gefühl der unendlichen Lebensfülle anregt. Die Natur ist organisch, und die höchste Schönheit daher immer und ewig vegetabilisch, und das gleiche gilt auch von der Moral und der Liebe.

> (*Athenäum Fragment*, No. 86, *Kritische Werke*, vol. II, p. 264.)

*   *   *   *   *

From the romantic point of view the most curious sorts of poetry, even the most eccentric and the monstrous, are of value as preliminary exercises to universality, provided there is in them some grain of originality.

Aus dem romantischen Gesichtspunkt haben auch die Abarten der Poesie, selbst die ekzentrischen und monströsen, ihren Wert, als Materialien und Vorübungen der Universalität, wenn nur irgendetwas drin ist, wenn sie nur original sind.

> (*Athenäum Fragment*, No. 139, *Kritische Ausgabe*, vol. II, p. 187.)

*   *   *   *   *

But the highest beauty, indeed the highest order is then ultimately only that of chaos, that is to say, a state awaiting the touch of love to unfold it into a harmonious universe, a state such as existed in ancient mythology and poetry. For mythology and poetry are one and indivisible. All the poems of Antiquity are linked one to another, until out of a growing agglomeration the whole is formed; everything is intertwined with all else, and everywhere one and the same spirit is expressed, only differently. And so it is truly no vacuous image to say: ancient poetry is a single, indivisible, perfect poem. Why should not that which already has been come into being again? In a different manner, of course. And why not a more beautiful, greater manner?

Aber die höchste Schönheit, ja die höchste Ordnung ist denn doch nur die des Chaos, nämlich eines solchen, welches nur auf die Berührung der Liebe wartet, um sich zu einer harmonischen Welt zu entfalten, eines solchen wie es auch die alte Mythologie und Poesie war. Denn Mythologie und Poesie, beide sind eins und unzertrennlich. Alle Gedichte des Altertums schliessen sich eines an das andre, bis sich aus immer grössern Massen und Gliedern das Ganze bildet; alles greift in einander, und überall ist ein und derselbe Geist nur anders ausgedrückt. Und so ist es wahrlich kein leeres Bild, zu sagen: die alte Poesie sei ein einziges, unteilbares, vollendetes Gedicht. Warum sollte nicht wieder von neuem werden, was schon gewesen ist? Auf eine andre Weise versteht sich. Und warum nicht auf eine schönere, grössere?

(*Gespräch über die Poesie*, *Kritische Ausgabe*, vol. II, p. 313.)

*   *   *   *   *

AUGUST WILHELM SCHLEGEL

According to Schelling, beauty is *the infinite portrayed in finite form*, a definition in which, as is fitting, the sublime is already included. I wholly concur with this, only I should prefer to put it this way: the beautiful is a symbolic representation of the infinite, for from this formulation it becomes clear how the infinite can appear in the finite. The infinite is not to be regarded as a philosophic fiction, nor to be sought beyond the world: it surrounds us on all sides, we can never escape it, we live, exist and are in the infinite. Admittedly we have its testimony only through reason and imagination; we can never grasp it with our senses and understanding, for these depend on a constant positing of the finite and denial of the infinite. The finite forms the

surface of our nature, otherwise we could have no firm existence: the infinite forms its basis, otherwise we should have
everywhere no reality.

How then can the infinite be brought to the surface, into
appearance? Only symbolically, in pictures and signs. The
unpoetic view of things is that which considers everything to be
dismissed through the perceptions of the senses and the findings
of our understanding; the poetic view is that which goes on for
ever interpreting them and sees in them an inexhaustible
fount of images. (Kant once speaks of the hieroglyphic writing
in which nature addresses us in images of its beautiful forms.)
Thereby everything comes alive to us. The creation of poetry
(taking this phrase in its widest sense to refer to all the arts) is
nothing other than an eternal process of symbolising: we either
seek an external form for the spiritual, or we relate the external
to something invisible and inward.

Nach Schelling ist *das Unendliche endlich dargestellt* Schönheit,
bei welcher Definition das Erhabene, wie es sich gehört, schon
darunter begriffen ist. Hiermit bin ich vollkommen einverstanden,
nur möchte ich den Ausdruck lieber so bestimmen: Das
Schöne ist eine symbolische Darstellung des Unendlichen;
weil alsdann zugleich klar wird, wie das Unendliche zur Erscheinung kommen kann. Man halte das Unendliche nicht etwa für
eine philosophische Fiktion, man suche es nicht jenseits der
Welt: es umgibt uns überall, wir können ihm niemals entgehen;
wir leben, weben und sind im Unendlichen. Freilich haben
wir seine Gewähr nur in unserer Vernunft und Phantasie; mit
den äusseren Sinnen und dem Verstande können wir es nie
ergreifen, denn diese bestehen eben nur durch ein beständiges
Setzen von Endlichkeiten und Verneinen des Unendlichen.
Das Endliche macht die Oberfläche unserer Natur aus, sonst
könnten wir keine bestimmte Existenz haben: das Unendliche
die Grundlage, sonst hätten wir überall keine Realität.
Wie kann nun das Unendliche auf die Oberfläche, zur Er-

scheinung gebracht werden? Nur symbolisch, in Bildern und Zeichen. Die unpoetische Ansicht der Dinge ist die, welche mit den Wahrnehmungen der Sinne und den Bestimmungen des Verstandes alles an ihnen für abgetan hält; die poetische, welche sie immerfort deutet und eine figürliche Unerschöpflichkeit in ihnen sieht. (Kant spricht einmal von der Chifferschrift, wodurch die Natur in ihren schönen Formen figürlich zu uns spricht.) Dadurch wird erst alles für uns lebendig. Dichten (im weitesten Sinne für das Poetische allen Künsten zum Grunde liegende genommen) ist nichts anderes als ein ewiges Symbolisieren: wir suchen entweder für etwas Geistiges eine äussere Hülle oder wir beziehen ein Äusseres auf ein unsichtbares Inneres.

(*Vorlesungen über schöne Kunst und Literatur, Kritische Schriften*, vol. VI, pp. 81–2.)

*   *   *   *   *

To be without form is certainly not permissible to the works of genius, but there is no danger of this. In order to parry the reproach of formlessness, let us try to comprehend the concept of form that is conceived by most critics, in their insistence on stiff regularity, as merely mechanical, and not, as it should be, in organic terms. Form is mechanical if it is imposed from without as a fortuitous addition unrelated to the object's essence; as a soft mass, for instance, is pressed into some shape which it retains on hardening. Organic form, on the other hand, is innate; it evolves from the inner being and attains its final predestined shape with the seed's maturity. Such forms may be seen throughout nature, wherever living forces are active, from the crystallisation of salts and minerals, through plants and flowers, right up to the formation of the human face. In the fine arts too, as in nature, that greatest of artists, every genuine form is organic, i.e. determined by the work's content. In short, form is nothing other than a meaningful exterior, the articulate physiognomy of each object, undisturbed by accidental intrusions, and therefore giving faithful testimony to the object's hidden essence.

Formlos zu sein darf also den Werken des Genius auf keine Weise gestattet werden, allein es hat damit auch keine Gefahr. Um dem Vorwurfe der Formlosigkeit zu begegnen, verständige man sich nur über den Begriff der Form, der von den meisten, namentlich von jenen Kunstrichtern, welche vor allem auf steife Regelmässigkeit dringen, nur mechanisch und nicht, wie er sollte, organisch gefasst wird. Mechanisch ist die Form, wenn sie durch äussre Einwirkung irgendeinen Stoffe bloss als zufällige Zutat, ohne Beziehung auf dessen Beschaffenheit erteilt wird, wie man z.B. einer weichen Masse eine beliebige Gestalt gibt, damit sie solche nach der Erhärtung beibehalte. Die organische Form hingegen ist eingeboren, sie bildet von innen heraus und erreicht ihre Bestimmtheit zugleich mit der vollständigen Entwicklung des Keimes. Solche Formen entdecken wir in der Natur überall, wo sich lebendige Kräfte regen, von der Kristallisation der Salze und Mineralien an bis zur Pflanze und Blume und von dieser bis zur menschlichen Gesichtsbildung hinauf. Auch in der schönen Kunst, wie im Gebiete der Natur, der höchsten Künstlerin, sind alle echten Formen organisch, d.h. durch den Gehalt des Kunstwerkes bestimmt. Mit einem Worte, die Form ist nichts anders als ein bedeutsames Äussres, die sprechende, durch keine störenden Zufälligkeiten entstellte Physiognomie jedes Dinges, die von dessen verborgnem Wesen ein wahrhaftes Zeugnis ablegt.

(*Vorlesungen über dramatische Kunst und Literatur*,
Kritische Schriften, vol. VI, pp. 109–10.)

*   *   *   *   *

SAMUEL TAYLOR COLERIDGE

The safest definition, then, of Beauty, as well as the oldest, is that of Pythagoras: THE REDUCTION OF MANY TO ONE – or, as finely expressed by the sublime disciple of Ammonius, τὺ ἄμεπες ὄν, ἐν πολλοῖς Φανταζόμενον, of which the following may be offered as both paraphrase and corollary. *The sense of beauty subsists in simultaneous intuition of the relation of parts, each to each, and of all to a whole: exciting an immediate and absolute complacency, without intervenence, therefore, of any interest, sensual or intellectual.* The BEAUTIFUL is thus at once distinguished both from the AGREEABLE, which is beneath it, and from the GOOD, which is above it: for both these have an interest necessarily attached to them: both act on the WILL, and excite a desire for the actual existence of the image or idea contemplated: while the sense of beauty rests gratified in the mere contemplation or intuition, regardless whether it be a fictitious Apollo, or a real Antinous.

> (*On the Principles of Genial Criticism*, *Biographia Literaria*, vol. II, pp. 238–9.)

* * * * *

The GOOD consists in the congruity of a thing with the laws of the reason and the nature of the will, and in its fitness to determine the latter to actualize the former: and it is always discursive. The Beautiful arises from the perceived harmony of an object, whether sight or sound, with the inborn and constitutive rules of the judgement and imagination: and it is always intuitive. As light to the eye, even such is beauty to the mind, which cannot but have complacency in whatever is perceived as pre-configured to its living faculties.

> (*On the Principles of Genial Criticism*, *Biographia Literaria*, vol. II, p. 243.)

VICTOR HUGO

Just compare the royal garden at Versailles, well contoured, well pruned, well tended, well raked, well gravelled, full of little waterfalls, little ponds, little groves, bronze tritons ceremoniously frolicking on seas pumped at great expense from the Seine, marble fauns paying court to the druids allegorically framed by a host of conical yew-trees, cylindrical laurels, spherical orange-trees, elliptical myrtles, and other trees whose natural shape had undoubtedly been deemed too trivial and that had been gracefully corrected by the gardener's shears; compare this highly acclaimed garden with a primitive forest in the New World with its giant trees, high grasses, dense vegetation, thousands of multi-coloured birds, broad trails where shade and light play upon the greenery, wild harmonies, great rivers bearing islands of flowers, immense cataracts crowned by rainbows! We shall not ask: Where is the magnificence? where is the grandeur? or where is the beauty? but simply: Where is the order? where is the disorder? There, captive waters diverted from their course, gushing forth only to stagnate; petrified deities; trees transplanted from their native soil, torn from their climate, deprived even of their natural form, of their fruits, and forced to submit to the grotesque caprices of the clippers and straighteners; in short, everywhere the natural order is contravened, inverted, overturned, destroyed. Here, by contrast, everything obeys an immutable law; a God seems to dwell in everything. The drops of water follow their natural course, forming rivers which will make seas; the seeds choose their own terrain and produce a forest. Every plant, every shrub, every tree springs up in its season, grows in its place, bears its fruit, and dies in its time. Even the briar is beautiful. Still we ask: Where is the order?

So choose between the gardener's masterpiece and the work of nature, between conventional beauty and a beauty devoid of rules, between an artificial literature and poetry of originality!

The objection will be raised, that the virgin forest hides within its secluded splendours thousands of dangerous beasts, and that the stagnant lakes of the French garden conceal at most a few insipid animals. That is, no doubt, unfortunate; but all things considered, we like a crocodile better than a toad; we prefer a barbarism by Shakespeare to an ineptitude by Campistron.

It is very important to establish that in literature, as in politics, order is marvellously compatible with freedom; it is even its outcome. Moreover, one must be careful not to confuse order with regularity. Regularity is concerned only with outer form; order springs from the very essence of things, from the meaningful arrangement of the innermost elements of a subject. Regularity is a purely human and material schema; order is, so to speak, divine. These two aspects, so diverse in character, often go their separate ways. A Gothic cathedral shows an admirable order in its naive irregularity; our modern French buildings, to which Greek and Roman architectural styles have been so ineptly applied, offer us only a regular disorder. Any man will always be able to produce a regular piece of work; it is only great minds who know how to shape a composition. The creator, from on high, shapes; the imitator, from close range, systematises; the former follows the laws of his nature, the latter the rules of his school. Art is a matter of inspiration for the one, and merely an exercise for the other. To sum up – and we do not object to judging according to this observation the two literatures called *classical* and *romantic* – regularity is the taste of mediocrity, order is the taste of genius.

Comparez un moment au jardin royal de Versailles, bien nivelé, bien taillé, bien nettoyé, bien ratissé, bien sablé, tout plein de petites cascades, de petits bassins, de petits bosquets, de tritons de bronze folâtrant en cérémonie sur des océans pompés à grands frais dans la Seine, de faunes de marbre courtisant les dryades allégoriquement renfermées dans une multitude d'ifs coniques, de lauriers cylindriques, d'orangers sphériques, de myrtes elliptiques, et d'autres arbres dont la forme naturelle, trop triviale sans doute, a été gracieusement corrigée par la serpette du jardinier; comparez ce jardin si vanté à une forêt primitive du Nouveau-Monde, avec ses arbres géants, ses hautes herbes, sa végétation profonde, ses mille oiseaux de mille couleurs, ses larges avenues où l'ombre et la lumière ne se jouent que sur de la verdure, ses sauvages harmonies, ses grands fleuves qui charrient des îles de fleurs, ses immenses cataractes qui balancent des arcs-en-ciel! Nous ne dirons pas: Où est la magnificence? où est la grandeur? où est la beauté? mais simplement: Où est l'ordre? où est le désordre? Là, des eaux captives ou détournées de leur cours, ne jaillissant que pour croupir; des dieux pétrifiés; des arbres transplantés de leur sol natal, arrachés de leur climat, privés même de leur forme, de leurs fruits, et forcés de subir les grotesques caprices de la serpe et du cordeau; partout enfin l'ordre naturel contrarié, interverti, bouleversé, détruit. Ici, au contraire, tout obéit à une loi invariable; un Dieu semble vivre en tout. Les gouttes d'eau suivent leur pente et font des fleuves, qui feront des mers; les semences choisissent leur terrain et produisent une forêt. Chaque plante, chaque arbuste, chaque arbre naît dans sa saison, croît en son lieu, produit son fruit, meurt à son temps. La ronce même y est belle. Nous le demandons encore: Où est l'ordre?

Choisissez donc du chef-d'œuvre du jardinage ou de l'œuvre de la nature, de ce qui est beau de convention ou de ce qui est beau sans les règles, d'une littérature artificielle ou d'une poésie originale!

On nous objectera que la forêt vierge cache dans ses magnifiques solitudes mille animaux dangereux, et que les bassins marécageux du jardin français recèlent tout au plus quelques bêtes insipides. C'est un malheur sans doute; mais, à tout prendre, nous aimons mieux un crocodile qu'un crapaud; nous préférons une barbarie de Shakespeare à une ineptie de Campistron.

Ce qu'il est très important de fixer, c'est qu'en littérature comme en politique l'ordre se concilie merveilleusement avec la liberté; il en est même le résultat. Au reste, il faut bien se garder de confondre l'ordre avec la régularité. La régularité ne s'attache qu'à la forme extérieure; l'ordre résulte du fond même des choses, de la disposition intelligente des éléments intimes d'un sujet. La régularité est une combinaison matérielle et purement humaine; l'ordre est pour ainsi dire divin. Ces deux qualités si diverses dans leur essence marchent fréquemment l'une sans l'autre. Une cathédrale gothique présente un ordre admirable dans sa naïve irrégularité; nos édifices français modernes, auxquels on a si gauchement appliqué l'architecture grecque ou romaine, n'offrent qu'un désordre régulier. Un homme ordinaire pourra toujours faire un ouvrage régulier; il n'y a que les grands esprits qui sachent ordonner une composition. Le créateur, qui voit de haut, ordonne; l'imitateur, qui regarde de près, régularise; le premier procède selon la loi de sa nature, le dernier suivant les règles de son école. L'art est une inspiration pour l'un; il n'est qu'une science pour l'autre. En deux mots, et nous ne nous opposons pas à ce qu'on juge d'après cette observation les deux littératures dites *classique* et *romantique*, la régularité est le goût de la médiocrité, l'ordre est le goût du génie.

(1826 Preface to *Odes et Ballades*, *Œuvres poétiques*, vol. 1, pp. 280–2.)

*   *   *   *   *

So here is a new religion, a new society; on this dual foundation we must see a new poetry grow. Until then – and let the reader forgive me for stating a conclusion he must already have drawn himself from the foregoing remarks – until then, under the influence of polytheism and ancient philosophy, the Ancients' purely epic muse had studied nature only under a single aspect, mercilessly banishing from art all that did not conform to a certain prototype of beauty in a world dominated by imitation. It was a magnificent prototype at the outset, but as always happens with any system, it latterly became petty, artificial, and conventional. Christianity leads poetry to truth. Like Christianity, the modern muse will see things from a higher and wider perspective. She will realise that not all of creation is *beautiful* in human terms, that the ugly exists alongside the beautiful, the misshapen beside the graceful, the grotesque as the obverse of the sublime, evil with good, dark with light. She will ask whether the artist's restricted and relative reason should have priority over the creator's infinite, absolute reason; whether it is for man to rectify God; whether a mutilated nature will be more beautiful; whether art has the right, as it were, to reduplicate man, life and creation; whether a thing will work better when its muscles and its mainspring have been removed; whether, in short, incompleteness is the means to harmony. It is, then, in the light of events both ridiculous and daunting, and under the impact of that Christian melancholy and philosophical criticism just noted, that poetry will take a great step, a decisive step, a step which, like the jolt of an earthquake, will change the entire face of the intellectual world. Poetry will begin to do like nature, to mingle, but not fuse, in her creations darkness with light, the grotesque with the sublime, in other words, the body with the soul, the animal with the spirit; for the point of departure for religion is always that for poetry too.

So we have a new principle unknown to Antiquity, a new prototype introduced into poetry; and since a factor added to being modifies the whole being, we have a new form developing in art. That prototype is the grotesque; that form is comedy.

And let me underscore this; for we have just pinpointed the characteristic feature, the fundamental difference dividing, in our opinion, modern art from ancient art, real form from dead form, or to use vaguer but more current terms, *romantic* literature from *classical* literature.

[. .]

In the thought of the Moderns, by contrast, the grotesque plays an immense role. It is everywhere; on the one hand, it creates the horrible and the misshapen; on the other, the comical and the farcical. It clusters around religion a multitude of new superstitions, around poetry a multitude of picturesque inventions. It is the grotesque that abundantly scatters into air, water, earth and fire those myriads of indeterminate beings that we find with such vividness in the popular traditions of the Middle Ages; it is the grotesque that makes the frightening ring of the witches' Sabbath writhe in the dark, and that gives Satan his horns, his cloven feet, his batwings. It is the grotesque again that casts into Christian hell those hideous faces conjured up by the astringent genius of Dante and Milton, or that fills it with those preposterous forms, the delight of Callot, that burlesque Michaelangelo. Moving from the ideal to the real world, the grotesque unfurls endless parodies of humanity. Among the creations of its fantasy are those Scaramouches, Crispins and Harlequins, grimacing outlines of man wholly unknown to solemn Antiquity, yet emerging nonetheless from classical Italy. Finally, it is the grotesque, clothing the same drama in the imagination of the South and that of the North, that has Sganarelle gambol around Don Juan and Mephistopheles prowl around Faust.

[. .]

Beauty has only a single prototype, the ugly a thousand. It is because beauty, to put it in human terms, is just form in its simplest relationship, its highest consonance, its closest cohesion to our own structure. Consequently, it always affords a harmonious whole, though it is finite, like ourselves. What we call the ugly, by contrast, is a detail of a great conglomeration that eludes us and that harmonises not with man, but with creation in its entirety: that is why it constantly offers us new, open-ended views.

[. .]

It would be superfluous to dwell any further on the impact of the grotesque on the third phase of civilisation. In the epoch called *romantic*, everything attests to its intimate and creative union with the beautiful. Everything, down to the most naïve popular legends, illuminates with unerring instinct this mystery of modern art. Antiquity would not have produced *Beauty and the Beast*.

Voilà donc une nouvelle religion, une société nouvelle; sur cette double base, il faut que nous voyions grandir une nouvelle poésie. Jusqu'alors, et qu'on nous pardonne d'exposer un résultat que de lui-même le lecteur a déjà dû tirer de ce qui a été dit plus haut, jusqu'alors, agissant en cela comme le polythéisme et la philosophie antique, la muse purement épique des Anciens n'avait étudié la nature que sous une seule face, rejetant sans pitié de l'art presque tout ce qui, dans le monde soumis à son imitation, ne se rapportait pas à un certain type du beau. Type d'abord magnifique, mais, comme il arrive toujours de ce qui est systématique, devenu dans le derniers temps faux, mesquin et conventionnel. Le christianisme amène la poésie à la vérité. Comme lui, la muse moderne verra les choses d'un coup d'œil plus haut et plus large. Elle sentira que tout dans la création n'est pas humainement *beau*, que le laid y existe à côté du beau, le difforme près du gracieux, le grotesque au revers du sublime, le mal avec le bien, l'ombre avec la lumière. Elle se demandera si la raison étroite et relative de l'artiste doit avoir gain de cause sur la raison infinie, absolue, du créateur; si c'est à l'homme à rectifier Dieu; si une nature mutilée en sera plus belle; si l'art a le droit de dédoubler, pour ainsi dire, l'homme, la vie, la création; si chaque chose marchera mieux quand on lui aura ôté son muscle et son ressort; si, enfin, c'est le moyen d'être harmonieux que d'être incomplet. C'est alors que, l'œil fixé sur des événements tout à la fois risibles et formidables, et sous l'influence de cet esprit de mélancolie chrétienne et de critique philosophique que nous observions tout à l'heure, la poésie fera un grand pas, un pas décisif, un pas qui, pareil à la secousse d'un

tremblement de terre, changera toute la face du monde intellec-
tuel. Elle se mettra à faire comme la nature, à mêler dans ses
créations, sans pourtant les confondre, l'ombre à la lumière, le
grotesque au sublime, en d'autres termes, le corps à l'âme, la
bête à l'esprit; car le point de départ de la religion est toujours
le point de départ de la poésie. Tout se tient.

Ainsi voilà un principe étranger à l'Antiquité, un type
nouveau introduit dans la poésie; et, comme une condition de
plus dans l'être modifie l'être tout entier, voilà une forme
nouvelle qui se développe dans l'art. Ce type, c'est le grotesque.
Cette forme, c'est la comédie.

Et ici, qu'il nous soit permis d'insister; car nous venons
d'indiquer le trait caractéristique, la différence fondamentale
qui sépare, à notre avis, l'art moderne de l'art antique, la forme
actuelle de la forme morte, ou, pour nous servir de mots plus
vagues, mais plus accrédités, la littérature *romantique* de la
littérature *classique*.

[. . .]

Dans la pensée des Modernes, au contraire, le grotesque a un
rôle immense. Il y est partout; d'une part, il crée le difforme et
l'horrible; de l'autre, le comique et le bouffon. Il attache autour
de la religion mille superstitions originales, autour de la poésie
mille imaginations pittoresques. C'est lui qui sème à pleines mains
dans l'air, dans l'eau, dans la terre, dans le feu, ces myriades
d'êtres intermédiaires que nous retrouvons tout vivants dans les
traditions populaires du Moyen Age; c'est lui qui fait tourner
dans l'ombre la ronde effrayante du sabbat, lui encore qui donne
à Satan les cornes, les pieds de bouc, les ailes de chauve-souris.
C'est lui, toujours lui, qui tantôt jette dans l'enfer chrétien ces
hideuses figures qu'évoquera l'âpre génie de Dante et de Milton, tantôt le peuple de ces formes ridicules au milieu desquelles
se jouera Callot, le Michel-Ange burlesque. Si du monde idéal il
passe au monde réel, il y déroule d'intarissables parodies de
l'humanité. Ce sont des créations de sa fantaisie que ces
Scaramouches, ces Crispins, ces Arlequins, grimaçantes

silhouettes de l'homme, types tout à fait inconnus à la grave Antiquité, et sortis pourtant de la classique Italie. C'est lui enfin qui, colorant tour à tour le même drame de l'imagination du Midi et de l'imagination du Nord, fait gambader Sganarelle autour de don Juan et ramper Méphistophélès autour de Faust.

[. . .]

Le beau n'a qu'un type; le laid en a mille. C'est que le beau, à parler humainement, n'est que la forme considérée dans son rapport le plus simple, dans sa symétrie la plus absolue, dans son harmonie la plus intime avec notre organisation. Aussi nous offre-t-il toujours un ensemble complet, mais restreint comme nous. Ce que nous appelons le laid, au contraire, est un détail d'un grand ensemble qui nous échappe, et qui s'harmonise, non pas avec l'homme, mais avec la création tout entière. Voilà pourquoi il nous présente sans cesse des aspects nouveaux, mais incomplets.

[. . .]

Il serait surabondant de faire ressortir davantage cette influence du grotesque dans la troisième civilisation. Tout démontre, à l'époque dite *romantique*, son alliance intime et créatrice avec le beau. Il n'y a pas jusqu'aux plus naïves légendes populaires qui n'expliquent quelquefois avec un admirable instinct ce mystère de l'art moderne. L'Antiquité n'aurait pas fait la *Belle et la Bête*.

(*Préface de 'Cromwell'*, pp. 68–75.)

PART III
ROMANTIC ART: FORM AND GENRE

MINGLING OF FORM

FRIEDRICH SCHLEGEL

Should poetry simply be divided up? Or should it remain one and indivisible? Or alternate between separation and cohesion? Most conceptions of the poetic world system are still as uncouth and childish as the old astronomical concepts before Copernicus. The customary divisions of poetry are only a dead framework for a limited horizon. What can be done, or what is just then accepted, is the static earth at the centre. But in the universe of poetry itself, nothing is static, everything is becoming and changing and moving harmoniously; and comets too have immutable laws of movement. However, so long as the course of these stars cannot be calculated, nor their return predicted, the true universal system of poetry is not yet discovered.

Soll denn die Poesie schlechthin eingeteilt sein? oder soll sie die eine und unteilbare bleiben? oder wechseln zwischen Trennung und Verbindung? Die meisten Vorstellungsarten vom poetischen Weltsystem sind noch so roh und kindisch, wie die ältern vom astronomischen vor Kopernikus. Die gewöhnlichen Einteilungen der Poesie sind nur totes Fachwerk für einen beschränkten Horizont. Was einer machen kann, oder was eben gilt, ist die ruhende Erde im Mittelpunkt. Im Universum der Poesie selbst aber ruht nichts, alles wird und verwandelt sich und bewegt sich harmonisch; und auch die Kometen haben unabänderliche Bewegungsgesetze. Ehe sich aber der Lauf dieser Gestirne nicht berechnen, ihre Wiederkunft nicht vorherbestimmen lässt, ist das wahre Weltsystem der Poesie noch nicht entdeckt.

(*Athenäum Fragment*, No. 434, *Kritische Ausgabe*, vol. II, p. 252.)

AUGUST WILHELM SCHLEGEL

I spoke in the first lecture about the origins and essence of the romantic, and I want here only to recall a few points. Ancient art and poetry aims at a stringent separation of what is unlike; the romantic delights in indissoluble mixtures; it fuses all contraries most intimately, nature and art, poetry and prose, the serious and the jocular, remembrance and foreboding, the spiritual and the sensual, the earthly and the divine, life and death. Just as the ancient law-makers dispensed their ordering precepts and laws in measured strains; this was already celebrated in a fable by Orpheus, the first to tame an as yet wild mankind; so the whole of ancient poetry is, as it were, a rhythmic nomos, a harmonious proclamation of a beautifully ordered world, resting on a permanently established set of laws and reflecting the eternal, primal images of things. Romantic poetry, on the other hand, is the expression of the secret urge towards the chaos that is constantly labouring to bring forth new and wonderful creations, and that is hidden beneath, indeed within, the orderly universe: the animating spirit of original love here floats anew over the waters. Ancient poetry is simpler, clearer, and more like nature in the independent completeness of its individual works; romantic poetry, in spite of its fragmentary appearance, is closer to the secret of the universe.

Über den Ursprung und das Wesen des Romantischen sprach ich in der ersten Vorlesung und will hier nur weniges in Erinnerung bringen. Die antike Kunst und Poesie geht auf strenge Sonderung des Ungleichartigen, die romantische gefällt sich in unauflöslichen Mischungen; alle Entgegengesetzten, Natur und Kunst, Poesie und Prosa, Ernst und Scherz, Erinnerung und Ahnung, Geistigkeit und Sinnlichkeit, das Irdische und Göttliche, Leben und Tod, verschmilzt sie auf das innigste miteinander. Wie die ältesten Gesetzgeber ihre ordnenden Lehren und Vorschriften in abgemessenen Weisen erteilten; wie dies schon vom Orpheus, dem ersten Besänftiger des noch wilden Menschengeschlechts, fabelhaft gerühmt wird: so ist die gesamte alte Poesie und Kunst gleichsam ein rhythmischer Nomos, eine harmonische Verkündigung der auf immer festgestellten Gesetzgebung einer schön geordneten und die ewigen Urbilder der Dinge in sich abspiegelnden Welt. Die romantische hingegen ist der Ausdruck des geheimen Zuges zu dem immerfort nach neuen und wundervollen Geburten ringenden Chaos, welches unter der geordneten Schöpfung, ja in ihrem Schosse sich verbirgt: der beseelende Geist der ursprünglichen Liebe schwebt hier von neuem über den Wassern. Jene ist einfacher, klarer, und der Natur in der selbständigen Vollendung ihrer einzelnen Werke ähnlicher; diese, ungeachtet ihres fragmentarischen Ansehens, ist dem Geheimnis des Weltalls näher.

(*Vorlesungen über dramatische Kunst und Literatur*,
Kritische Schriften, vol. VI, pp. 111–12.)

PERCY BYSSHE SHELLEY

The distinction between poets and prose writers is a vulgar error.

(*A Defence of Poetry, Complete Works*, vol. VII,
p. 114.)

VICTOR HUGO

Let us then state it boldly. The time has come, and it would be strange if in this epoch freedom, like light, would reach everywhere except the most innately free area in the world, the realm of thought. Let us hack up the theories, poetics, and systems. Let us tear down this old plaster which masks the facade of art! There are neither rules nor models; or rather, there are no rules other than the general laws of nature which determine the whole of art, and the special laws for each composition that spring from the conditions appropriate to each subject.

[. . .]

The poet, let us emphasise this point, must take counsel only from nature, from truth, and from inspiration, which is also a truth and a nature.

[. . .]

It is the primal sources that must be tapped. It is the same sap, diffused in the ground that nourishes all the trees in the forest, however different in shape, fruits and foliage they may be. It is the same nature that engenders and nurtures the most different geniuses. The true poet is a tree which can be lashed by all the winds and soaked by all the dew, but which bears his works like fruits, just as the *fabulist* bore his fables. What is the point of adhering to a master? of clinging to a model?

Disons-le donc hardiment. Le temps en est venu, et il serait étrange qu'à cette époque, la liberté, comme la lumière, pénétrât partout, excepté dans ce qu'il y a de plus nativement libre au monde, les choses de la pensée. Mettons le marteau dans les théories, les poétiques et les systèmes. Jetons bas ce vieux plâtrage qui masque la façade de l'art! Il n'y a ni règles, ni modèles; ou plutôt il n'y a d'autres règles que les lois générales de la nature qui planent sur l'art tout entier, et les lois spéciales qui, pour chaque composition, résultent des conditions d'existence propres à chaque sujet.

[. .]

Le poète, insistons sur ce point, ne doit donc prendre conseil que de la nature, de la vérité, et de l'inspiration qui est aussi une vérité et une nature.

[. .]

Il faut puiser aux sources primitives. C'est la même sève, répandue dans le sol, qui produit tous les arbres de la forêt, si divers de port, de fruits, de feuillage. C'est la même nature qui féconde et nourrit les génies les plus différents. Le vrai poète est un arbre qui peut être battu de tous les vents et abreuvé de toutes les rosées, qui porte ses ouvrages comme ses fruits, comme le *fablier* portait ses fables. A quoi bon s'attacher à un maître? se greffer sur un modèle?

(*Préface de 'Cromwell'*, pp. 88–9.)

DRAMA

AUGUST WILHELM SCHLEGEL

The similarity between the English and the Spanish theatre resides not only in the audacious neglect of the unities of time and place, and in the mingling of comic and tragic elements: these could still be regarded as merely negative features, i.e. that they would not, or could not, comply with the rules and with reason (synonymous terms in the opinion of certain critics). The similarity, indeed, resides much deeper in the innermost substance of the works and in their fundamental configurations which make iconoclastic form a real necessity, so that its validity is also the source of its significance. What they have in common is the spirit of romantic poetry, in the context of drama. But – to keep matters within their proper perspective – in our view, the Spanish theatre is almost wholly romantic until its decline since the beginning of the eighteenth century; whereas the English theatre is romantic to perfection only in its founder and greatest master, Shakespeare.

Die Ähnlichkeit des englischen und spanischen Theaters besteht nicht bloss in der kühnen Vernachlässigung der Einheiten von Ort und von Zeit und in der Vermischung komischer und tragischer Bestandteile: was man immer noch als bloss verneinende Eigenheiten betrachten könnte, dass sie sich nämlich nicht nach den Regeln und der Vernunft (in der Meinung gewisser Kunstrichter gleichbedeutende Wörter) hätten fügen wollen oder können; sondern sie liegt weit tiefer im innersten Gehalt der Dichtungen und in den wesentlichen Beziehungen, wodurch jene abweichende Form ein wahres Erfordernis wird, die mit ihrer Gültigkeit zugleich ihre Bedeutung erhält. Was sie miteinander gemein haben, ist der Geist der romantischen Poesie, dramatisch ausgesprochen. Doch damit wir uns gleich mit der gehörigen Einschränkung erklären, so ist unsers Erachtens das spanische Theater bis zu seinem Verfall seit dem Anfange des achzehnten Jahrhunderts fast durchgehends romantisch; das englische ist es nur in seinem Stifter und grössten Meister, Shakespeare, auf vollkommne Weise.

(*Vorlesungen über dramatische Kunst und Literatur*, *Kritische Schriften*, vol. VI, p. III.)

*   *   *   *   *

In regard to the poetic genre under consideration here, we compared Ancient tragedy to a group in sculpture: the figures correspond to the characters, their grouping to the action, and on this the entire attention is centred, in both genres of this type of art, as the exclusive focus. Romantic drama, by contrast, should be conceived as a vast painting in which, besides the figure and movement in richer groups, the characters' surroundings are portrayed too, not only the immediate surroundings, but also a commanding view into the distance, and all this in a magic illumination which helps to evoke a particular impression.

Such a picture will be less perfectly delimited than the group, for it is like a fragment cut out of the optical world-stage. However, the painter will know how to fix our gaze appropriately through the framing of the foreground, the concentration of light in the centre, and by other means so that it does not stray out beyond what is represented, nor miss anything.

In the representation of the figure, painting cannot compete with sculpture because painting perceives it only through an illusion and from a single angle; on the other hand, it lends greater vivacity to its imitations through colour, which it can use in the subtlest gradations of spiritual expression, particularly in the faces. Through the look in the eyes, which sculpture can never fully convey, painting can also read further into the mind and see its slightest stirrings. Its real magic lies ultimately in its ability to make visible the least corporeal aspect of corporeal objects, i.e. light and air.

Just this kind of beauty is peculiar to romantic drama. It does not, like ancient tragedy, single out the serious and action from among the components of life; it embraces its whole lively spectacle and all its circumstances, and while it seems to portray only random relationships, it satisfies the subconscious demands of the imagination, draws us into contemplation of the mysterious significance of the tableau that has been harmonised through order, distance and closeness, colouring and lighting, and so, as it were, lends soul to the prospect.

The variety of times and places, provided its effect on the mind is also included, and that it is relevant to the theatrical perspective, to what is indicated in the distance or half-concealed by intervening objects; the contrast of levity and seriousness, provided they maintain due proportion in degree and kind; finally, the mixture of dialogue and lyricism, whereby the poet can transform his characters into more or less poetic beings: these are, in my opinion, not just licences of romantic drama, but its true beauties. In all these aspects, and in many others, we shall find complete similarity between the English and Spanish works that really deserve the name romantic, however great their divergence in other respects.

Was nun die dichterische Gattung betrifft, womit wir uns hier beschäftigen, so verglichen wir die antike Tragödie mit einer Gruppe in der Skulptur, die Figuren entsprechen dem Charakter, ihre Gruppierung der Handlung, und hierauf ist, als auf das einzige Dargestellte, die Betrachtung bei beiden Arten von Kunstwerken ausschliesslich gerichtet. Das romantische Drama denke man sich hingegen als ein grosses Gemälde, wo ausser der Gestalt und Bewegung in reichern Gruppen auch noch die Umgebung der Personen mitabgebildet ist, nicht bloss die nächste, sondern ein bedeutender Ausblick in die Ferne, und dies alles unter einer magischen Beleuchtung, welche den Eindruck so oder anders bestimmen hilft.

Ein solches Gemälde wird weniger vollkommen begrenzt sein als die Gruppe, denn es ist wie ein ausgeschnittenes Bruchstück aus dem optischen Schauplatze der Welt. Indessen wird der Maler durch die Einfassung der Vorgründe, durch das gegen die Mitte gesammelte Licht und andre Mittel den Blick gehörig festzuhalten wissen, dass er weder über die Darstellung hinausschweife, noch etwas in ihr vermisse.

In der Abbildung der Gestalt kann die Malerei nicht mit der Skulptur wetteifern, weil jene sie nur durch eine Täuschung und aus einem einzigen Gesichtspunkt auffasst; dagegen erteilt sie ihren Nachahmungen mehr Lebendigkeit durch die Farbe, die sie besonders in den feinsten Abstufungen des geistigen Ausdrucks in den Gesichtern zu benutzen weiss. Auch lässt sie durch den Blick, welchen die Skulptur doch immer nur unvollkommen geben kann, weit tiefer im Gemüt lesen und dessen leiseste Regungen vernehmen. Ihr eigentlicher Zauber liegt endlich darin, dass sie an körperlichen Gegenständen sichtbar macht, was am wenigsten körperlich, ist, Licht und Luft.

Gerade dergleichen Schönheiten sind dem romantischen Drama eigentümlich. Es sondert nicht strenge, wie die alte Tragödie, den Ernst und die Handlung unter den Bestandteilen des Lebens aus; es fasst das ganze bunte Schauspiel desselben mit allen Umgebungen zusammen, und indem es nur das zufällig nebeneinander Befindliche abzubilden scheint, befriedigt es die unbewussten Forderungen der Phantasie, vertieft uns in Betrachtungen über die unaussprechliche Bedeutung des durch Anordnung, Nähe und Ferne, Kolorit und Beleuchtung harmonisch gewordnen Scheines und leiht gleichsam der Aussicht eine Seele.

Der Wechsel der Zeiten und Örter, vorausgesetzt, dass sein Einfluss auf die Gemüter mitgeschildert ist, und dass er der theatralischen Perspektive in Bezug auf das in der Ferne Angedeutete oder von deckenden Gegenständen halb Versteckte zustatten kommt; der Kontrast von Scherz und Ernst, vorausgesetzt, dass sie im Grade und der Art ein Verhältnis zueinander haben; endlich die Mischung der dialogischen und lyrischen Bestandteile, wodurch der Dichter es in der Gewalt hat, seine Personen mehr oder weniger in poetische Naturen zu verwandeln, sind nach meiner Ansicht im romantischen Drama nicht etwa blosse Lizenzen, sondern wahre Schönheiten. In allen diesen Punkten, und noch in manchen andern, werden wir die englischen und spanischen Werke, welche vorzugsweise diesen Namen verdienen, einander vollkommen ähnlich finden, wie weit sie auch sonst voneinander abstehen mögen.

(*Vorlesungen über dramatische Kunst und Literatur,*
Kritische Schriften, vol. VI, pp. 112–13.)

PERCY BYSSHE SHELLEY

The modern practice of blending comedy with tragedy,

though liable to great abuse in point of practice, is undoubtedly an extension of the dramatic circle.

(*A Defence of Poetry, Complete Works*, vol. VII, p. 120.)

STENDHAL

What is romantic tragedy?

I reply boldly: it is tragedy in prose that lasts several months and occurs in various places.

The poets, who cannot understand such difficult discussions, such as M. Viennet, and the people who do not want to understand, clamour for a *clear* concept. But, to my mind, nothing is clearer than this: *A romantic tragedy is written in prose, the sequence of events put before the spectators lasts several months, and occurs in different places.*

Qu'est-ce que la tragédie romantique?

Je réponds hardiment: C'est la tragédie en prose qui dure plusieurs mois et se passe en des lieux divers.

Les poètes qui ne peuvent pas comprendre ces sortes de discussions, fort difficiles, M. Viennet, par exemple, et les gens qui ne veulent pas comprendre, demandent à grands cris une idée *claire*. Or, il me semble que rien n'est plus clair que ceci: *Une tragédie romantique est écrite en prose, la succession des événements qu'elle presente aux yeux des spectateurs dure plusieurs mois, et ils se passent en des lieux différents.*

(*Racine et Shakespeare*, p. 105.)

*   *   *   *   *

Now that I have gone into lengthy explanations, I think I can state, with the hope of being understood by everyone, and of not being misconstrued, even by the *famous* M. Villemain: romanticism, as applied to the genre of tragedy, IS A TRAGEDY IN PROSE LASTING SEVERAL MONTHS AND OCCURRING IN VARIOUS PLACES.

A présent que je me suis expliqué fort au long, il me semble que je puis dire avec l'espoir d'être compris de tout le monde et l'assurance de n'être pas travesti même par le *célèbre* M. Villemain: le romantisme appliqué au genre tragique, C'EST UNE TRAGÉDIE EN PROSE QUI DURE PLUSIEURS MOIS ET SE PASSE EN DIVERS LIEUX.

(*Racine et Shakespeare*, p. 126.)

* * * * *

The romantics do not advocate a direct imitation of Shakespeare's plays.

What must be imitated from this great man is the approach to the world in which we live, and the art of giving our contemporaries exactly the sort of tragedy they need, but which they do not have the audacity to demand, overawed as they are by the reputation of the great Racine.

It so happens that the new French tragedy would be very like Shakespeare's.

Les romantiques ne conseillent à personne d'imiter directement les drames de Shakespeare.

Ce qu'il faut imiter de ce grand homme, c'est la manière d'étudier le monde au milieu duquel nous vivons, et l'art de donner à nos contemporains précisément le genre de tragédie dont ils ont besoin, mais qu'ils n'ont pas l'audace de réclamer, terrifiés qu'ils sont par la réputation du grand Racine.

Par hasard, la nouvelle tragédie française resemblerait beaucoup à celle de Shakespeare.

(*Racine et Shakespeare*, p. 69.)

VICTOR HUGO

Here we are now at the poetic summit of modern times. Shakespeare is drama; and drama, which blends in a single breath the grotesque and the sublime, the terrible and the farcical, tragedy and comedy, – drama is the mode appropriate to the third period of poetry, to contemporary literature.

So, to give a rapid summary of what has been said hitherto, poetry has three ages, each one corresponding to a social era: the ode, the epic, and the drama. Primitive times are lyrical, Ancient times epic, modern times dramatic. The ode celebrates eternity, the epic consecrates history, drama paints life. The essence of the first kind of poetry is naïvety, of the second simplicity, and of the third truthfulness.

Nous voici parvenus à la sommité poétique des temps modernes. Shakespeare, c'est le drame; et le drame, qui fond sous un même souffle le grotesque et le sublime, le terrible et le bouffon, la tragédie et la comédie, le drame est le caractère propre de la troisième époque de poésie, de la littérature actuelle.

Ainsi, pour résumer rapidement les faits que nous avons observés jusqu'ici, la poésie a trois âges, dont chacun correspond à une époque de la société: l'ode, l'épopée, le drame. Les temps primitifs sont lyriques, les temps antiques sont épiques, les temps modernes sont dramatiques. L'ode chante l'éternité, l'épopée solennise l'histoire, le drame peint la vie. Le caractère de la première poésie est la naïveté, le caractère de la seconde est la simplicité, le caractère de la troisième, la verité.

(*Préface de 'Cromwell'*, pp. 75–6.)

*　　*　　*　　*　　*

The poetry born of Christianity, the poetry of our times is, therefore, drama; the essence of drama is the real; the real stems from the organic combination of two modes, the sublime and the grotesque, which intersect in drama, as they do in life and creation. For true poetry, whole poetry resides in the harmony of opposites. Moreover, the time has come to state categorically – and here, in particular, the exceptions would confirm the rule – that everything in nature is in art.

La poésie née du christianisme, la poésie de notre temps est donc le drame; le caractère du drame est le réel; le réel résulte de la combinaison toute naturelle de deux types, le sublime et le grotesque, qui se croisent dans le drame, comme ils se croisent dans la vie et dans la création. Car la poésie vraie, la poésie complète, est dans l'harmonie des contraires. Puis, il est temps de le dire hautement, et c'est ici surtout que les exceptions confirmeraient la règle, tout ce qui est dans la nature est dans l'art.

(*Préface de 'Cromwell'*, p. 79.)

* * * * *

One sees how quickly the arbitrary distinction between genres crumbles in the face of reason and taste. The so-called rule of the two unities could be demolished with equal ease. We say two and not *three* unities, for the unity of action or of internal coherence, the only true and well-founded one, has for long been uncontested.

Eminent contemporaries, foreign and French alike, have already attacked this basic law of the pseudo-Aristotelian code in both practice and theory. In any case, the struggle could not be lengthy. At the first jolt, it cracked, so worm-eaten was this beam from the old shack of scholasticism!

What is strange, is that the old guard claims support for its rule of the two unities from the semblance of truth, whereas it is precisely the real that kills it. What indeed could be more improbable and more absurd than that forecourt, that peristyle, that antechamber, the insipid setting where our tragedies obligingly come to unfold, where conspirators turn up, mysteriously,

to rant against the tyrant, and then the tyrant to rant against the
conspirators, as if they were idyllically saying to each other:

Alternis cantemus: amant alterna Camenae.

Where has anyone seen a forecourt or peristyle of this sort?
What could be more contrary to what we shall not call truth,
since the scholastics make so little of it, but the semblance of
truth? As a result, anything that is too particular, too intimate,
too specific to take place in the antechamber or the square, i.e.
the entire drama, takes place in the wings. On the stage we see,
as it were, only the elbows of the action; the hands are elsewhere. Instead of action, we have narratives; instead of scenes,
descriptions.

On voit combien l'arbitraire distinction des genres croule vite
devant la raison et le goût. On ne ruinerait pas moins aisément la
prétendue règle des deux unités. Nous disons deux et non *trois*
unités, l'unité d'action ou d'ensemble, la seule vraie et fondée,
étant depuis longtemps hors de cause.

Des contemporains distingués, étrangers et nationaux, ont
déjà attaqué, et par la pratique et par la théorie, cette loi fondamentale du code pseudo-artistotélique. Au reste le combat ne
devait pas être long. A la première secousse elle a craqué, tant
était vermoulue cette solive de la vieille masure scolastique!

Ce qu'il y a d'étrange, c'est que les routiniers prétendent
appuyer leur règle des deux unités sur la vraisemblance, tandis
que c'est précisément le réel qui la tue. Quoi de plus
invraisemblable et de plus absurde en effet que ce vestibule, ce
péristyle, cette antichambre, lieu banal ou nos tragédies ont la
complaisance de venir se dérouler, où arrivent, on ne sait comment, les conspirateurs pour déclamer contre le tyran, le tyran
pour déclamer contre les conspirateurs, chacun à leur tour,
comme s'ils s'étaient dit bucoliquement:

Alternis cantemus; amant alterna Camenae.

Où a-t-on vu vestibule ou péristyle de cette sorte? Quoi de
plus contraire, nous ne dirons pas à la vérité, les scolastiques en

font bon marché, mais à la vraisemblance? Il résulte de là que tout ce qui est trop caractéristique, trop intime, trop local, pour se passer dans l'antichambre ou dans le carrefour, c'est-à-dire tout le drame, se passe dans la coulisse. Nous ne voyons en quelque sorte sur le théâtre que les coudes de l'action; ses mains sont ailleurs. Au lieu de scènes, nous avons des récits; au lieu de tableaux, des descriptions.

(Préface de 'Cromwell', pp. 81–2.)

* * * * *

It is beginning to be understood nowadays that the exact place is one of the basic elements of reality. The characters, speaking or acting, are not the only ones to impress the action on the spectator's mind. The place where a particular calamity has occurred becomes a terrible witness that cannot be dissociated from it; and the absence of this kind of silent character would, in drama, detract from the greatest scenes in history.

On commence à comprendre de nos jours que la localité exacte est un des premiers éléments de la réalité. Les personnages parlants ou agissants ne sont pas les seuls qui gravent dans l'esprit du spectateur la fidèle empreinte des faits. Le lieu où telle catastrophe s'est passée en devient un témoin terrible et inséparable; et l'absence de cette sorte de personnage muet décompléterait dans le drame les plus grandes scènes de l'histoire.

(Préface de 'Cromwell', p. 82.)

* * * * *

The unity of time is no sounder than the unity of place. To squeeze the action into twenty-four hours is as ridiculous as to squeeze it into a forecourt. Every action has its own duration, just as it has its special place. To give the same allocation of time to every happening! To use the same measure for everything! A cobbler who wanted to put the same shoes onto all feet would make us laugh. To criss-cross the unity of time with the unity of place, like the bars of a cage, and pedantically to push in – and in the name of Aristotle – all those happenings, those people, those images that providence so generously unfurls in the real world! It is a mutilation of men and of things, turning history into a grimace. Let me rather say: all this will die in the process; that is how the mutilating dogmatists arrive at their usual results: what was living in the chronicle is dead in the tragedy. And so, very often, the cage of the unities houses only a skeleton.

L'unité de temps n'est pas plus solide que l'unité de lieu. L'action, encadrée de force dans les vingt-quatre heures, est aussi ridicule qu'encadrée dans le vestibule. Toute action a sa durée propre comme son lieu particulier. Verser la même dose de temps à tous les événements! appliquer la même mesure sur tout! On rirait d'un cordonnier qui voudrait mettre le même soulier à tous les pieds. Croiser l'unité de temps à l'unité de lieu comme les barreaux d'une cage, et y faire pédantesquement entrer, de par Aristote, tous ces faits, tous ces peuples, toutes ces figures que la providence déroule à si grandes masses dans la réalité! c'est mutiler hommes et choses, c'est faire grimacer l'histoire. Disons mieux: tout cela mourra dans l'opération; et c'est ainsi que les mutilateurs dogmatiques arrivent à leur résultat ordinaire: ce qui était vivant dans la chronique est mort dans la tragédie. Voilà pourquoi, bien souvent, la cage des unités ne renferme qu'un squelette.

(*Préface de 'Cromwell'*, p. 83.)

*   *   *   *   *

To prove the absurdity of the rule of the two unities, one last reason would be enough. That is the existence of the third unity, the unity of action, the only one universally accepted because it has a factual basis: namely that neither the eye nor the human mind is able to grasp more than one complex at a time. This unity is as essential as the other two are superfluous. It is the unity of action that fixes the play's focus; thereby, in fact, it excludes the other two. There can no more be three unities in a play than three horizons in a picture. However, let us not mistake unity for simplicity of action. The unity of the whole does not in any way rule out subsidiary actions, which should buttress the main action. These parts, skilfully subordinated to the whole, must constantly point towards the central action and flank it at the different levels, on the various planes of the drama. The unity of the whole is the law of perspective in the theatre.

Il suffirait enfin, pour démontrer l'absurdité de la règle des deux unités, d'une dernière raison, prise dans les entrailles de l'art. C'est l'existence de la troisième unité, l'unité d'action, la seule admise de tous parce qu'elle résulte d'un fait: l'œil ni l'esprit humain ne sauraient saisir plus d'un ensemble à la fois. Celle-là est aussi nécessaire que les deux autres sont inutiles. C'est elle qui marque le point de vue du drame; or, par cela même, elle exclut les deux autres. Il ne peut pas plus y avoir trois unités dans le drame que trois horizons dans un tableau. Du reste, gardons-nous de confondre l'unité avec la simplicité d'action. L'unité d'ensemble ne répudie en aucune façon les actions secondaires sur lesquelles doit s'appuyer l'action principale. Il faut seulement que ces parties, savamment subordonnées au tout, gravitent sans cesse vers l'action centrale et se groupent autour d'elle aux différents étages ou plutôt sur les divers plans du drame. L'unité d'ensemble est la loi de perspective du théâtre.

(*Préface de 'Cromwell'*, p. 84.

*   *   *   *   *

One can realise that, in a work of this kind, if the poet must *select* (as indeed he must), he must select not the *beautiful*, but the *characteristic*. This does not mean to *produce* some *local colour*, as it is called nowadays, i.e. to add, as an afterthought, a few gaudy touches here and there to an otherwise spurious and conventional picture. It is not on the surface of the drama that the local colour should be, but in its depths, at the very heart of the work, whence it spreads outwards, of its own accord, spontaneously and evenly, so to say, into the play's every recess, like the sap rising from the root to the tree's furthest leaf. Drama should be steeped to the roots in this period colouring; it should, in a sense, be in its air, so that the change of century and of atmosphere is noticed only on entering and leaving.

On conçoit que, pour une œuvre de ce genre, si le poète doit *choisir* dans les choses (et il le doit), ce n'est pas le *beau*, mais le *caractéristique*. Non qu'il convienne de *faire*, comme on dit aujourd'hui, *de la couleur locale*, c'est-à-dire d'ajouter après coup quelques touches criardes çà et là sur un ensemble du reste parfaitement faux et conventionnel. Ce n'est point à la surface du drame que doit être la couleur locale, mais au fond, dans le cœur même de l'œuvre, d'où elle se répand au dehors, d'elle-même, naturellement, également, et, pour ainsi parler, dans tous les coins du drame, comme la sève qui monte de la racine à la dernière feuille de l'arbre. Le drame doit être radicalement imprégné de cette couleur des temps; elle doit en quelque sorte y être dans l'air, de façon qu'on ne s'aperçoive qu'en y entrant et qu'en en sortant qu'on a changé de siècle et d'atmosphère.

(*Préface de 'Cromwell'*, p. 91.)

* * * * *

Ultimately, whether a play is written in prose, or in verse, or in verse and prose, is only a secondary consideration. A work's rank must be decided not according to its form, but according to its intrinsic worth. In questions of this kind there is only one answer, only one weight that can tip the scale in art: that is genius.

Au reste, que le drame soit écrit en prose, qu'il soit écrit en vers, qu'il soit écrit en vers et en prose, ce n'est là qu'une question secondaire. La rang d'un ouvrage doit se fixer non d'après sa forme, mais d'après sa valeur intrinsèque. Dans des questions de ce genre, il n'y a qu'une solution; il n'y a qu'un poids qui puisse faire pencher la balance de l'art: c'est le génie.

(*Préface de 'Cromwell'*, p. 96.)

*   *   *   *   *

What is done nowadays? A spectator's enjoyment is divided into two separate parts. First he is given two hours of serious pleasure, then an hour of playful pleasure; making four hours in all, including the hour of interlude, which we do not count among the pleasures. What would romantic drama do? It would render down and artfully blend together these two kinds of pleasure. It would make the audience switch constantly from the grave to the droll, from buffoonish antics to harrowing emotions, *from the harsh to the gentle, from the amusing to the stern.* For, as we have already shown, drama is the grotesque with the sublime, the soul within the body, tragedy within comedy.

Que fait-on en effet maintenant? On divise les jouissances du spectateur en deux parts bien tranchées. On lui donne d'abord deux heures de plaisir sérieux, puis une heure de plaisir folâtre; avec l'heure d'entr'actes que nous ne comptons pas dans le plaisir, en tout quatre heures. Que ferait le drame romantique? Il broierait et mêlerait artistement ensemble ces deux espèces de plaisir. Il ferait passer à chaque instant l'auditoire du sérieux au rire, des excitations bouffonnes aux émotions déchirantes, *du grave au doux, du plaisant au sévère.* Car, ainsi que nous l'avons déjà établi, le drame, c'est le grotesque avec le sublime, l'âme sous le corps, c'est une tragédie sous une comédie.

(*Préface de 'Cromwell'*, p. 105.)

ALFRED DE VIGNY

Will the French stage, or will it not, open up to modern tragedy: – in scope, a broad panorama of life, instead of a limited picture of the final reckoning in a plot; – in composition, characters, not roles, tranquil, undramatic scenes side by side with comic and tragic ones; – in manner, a flexible style, comic, tragic, and at times epic?

[. .]

To begin with, bear in mind that, in the old system, every tragedy was a calamity, the denouement of an action already ripe when the curtain rose, hanging only by a thread, ready to drop. Thence stems that defect in French tragedies, as evident to you as to all foreigners: that paucity of scenes and of development, that artificial holding back, and then, that rush to wind up, together with the constant fear of lack of material to fill the five acts.

This will not be the way that the dramatic poet will work in the future. First of all, he will hold in his ample grasp a large expanse of time and will make whole lives move in it; he will create man, not as a *species*, but as an *individual* – the only way to interest humanity; he will let his creations live their own lives, and will merely sow in their hearts those seeds of passion from which great events must evolve; then, when the time has come, and only then, without any haste, he will show destiny tying its victims in a mass of inextricable knots. Then, far from finding his characters too small for the space, he will groan, he will cry out that he lacks air and room; for art will be just like life, and in life a major action brings an endless whirlwind of inevitable consequences in its wake.

[. .]

But a drama will never represent anything other than figures come together to speak to each other of their concerns; they must, therefore, speak. Let them be made to use that simple and direct *recitative*, of which Molière is the finest example in our language; when passion and misfortune inflame their hearts and exalt their thoughts, let the verse for a while rise to those sublime rhythms of passion that seem like a *song*, so powerfully do they sweep our souls aloft!

Does not everyone, in his usual speech, have favourite phrases, habitual words, rooted in his upbringing, his profession, his predilections, learned from his family, prompted by his innate loves and hates, by his bilious, sanguine or nervous temperament, determined by his heated or cold, calculating or frank turn of mind? Must then every figure use the same words, the same images that all the others use too? No, he must be brief or rambling, careless or precise, ornate or simple, according to his character, his age, his inclinations. Molière never failed to give these definite and revealing details, fruit of an attentive observation of mankind, and Shakespeare never dispenses an aphorism or an oath at random.

La scène française s'ouvrira-t-elle, ou non, à une tragédie moderne produisant: – dans sa conception, un tableau large de la vie, au lieu du tableau resserré de la catastrophe d'une intrigue; – dans sa composition, des caractères, non des rôles, des scènes paisibles sans drames, mêlées à des scènes comiques et tragiques; – dans son exécution un style familier, comique, tragique et parfois épique?

[. . .]

Considérez d'abord que, dans le système qui vient de s'éteindre, toute tragédie était une catastrophe et un dénoûment d'une action déjà mûre au lever du rideau, qui ne tenait plus qu'à un fil et n'avait plus qu'à tomber. De là est venu ce défaut qui vous frappe, ainsi que tous les étrangers, dans les tragédies françaises: cette parcimonie de scènes et de développements, ces faux retardements, et puis tout-à-coup cette hâte d'en finir, mêlée à cette crainte que l'on sent presque partout de manque d'étoffe pour remplir le cadre de cinq actes. . .

Ce ne sera pas ainsi qu'à l'avenir procédera le poète dramatique. D'abord il prendra dans sa large main beaucoup de temps et y fera mouvoir des existences entières; il créera l'homme, non comme *espèce*, mais comme *individu*, seul moyen d'intéresser à l'humanité; il laissera ses créatures vivre de leur propre vie, et jettera seulement dans leur cœur ces germes de passions par où se preparent les grands événements; puis, lorsque l'heure en sera venue, et seulement alors, sans que l'on sente que son doigt la hâte, il montrera la destinée enveloppant ses victimes dans des nœuds inextricables et multipliés. Alors, bien loin de trouver des personnages trop petits pour l'espace, il gémira, il s'écriera qu'il manque d'air et d'espace; car l'art sera tout semblable à la vie, et dans la vie une action principale entraîne autour d'elle un tourbillon de faits nécessaires et innombrables.

[. . .]

Mais un drame ne présentera jamais aux peuples que des personnages réunis pour se parler de leurs affaires; ils doivent donc parler. Que l'on fasse pour eux ce *récitatif* simple et franc dont Molière est le plus beau modèle dans notre langue; lorsque la passion et le malheur viendront animer leur cœur, élever leurs pensées, que le vers s'élève un moment jusqu'à ces mouvements sublimes de la passion qui semblent un *chant*, tant ils emportent nos âmes hors d'elles-mêmes!

Chaque homme, dans sa conversation habituelle, n'a-t-il pas ses formules favorites, ses mots coutumiers nés de son éducation, de sa profession, de ses goûts, appris en famille, inspirés par ses amours et ses aversions naturelles, par son tempérament bilieux, sanguin ou nerveux, dictés par un esprit passionné, ou froid, calculateur ou candide? . . . Faut-il donc toujours que chaque personnage se serve des mêmes mots, des mêmes images que tous les autres emploient aussi? Non, il doit être concis ou diffus, négligé ou calculé, prodigue ou avare d'ornements selon son caractère, son âge, ses penchants. Molière ne manqua jamais à donner ces touches fermes et franches qu'apprend l'observation attentive des hommes, et Shakespeare ne livre pas un proverbe, un juron au hasard.

('Lettre à Lord xxx', *Le More de Venise*, *Œuvres complètes*, vol. I, pp. 280–9.)

NARRATIVE

NOVALIS

Poetics: In the fable I think I am best able to express my spirit's mood. (Everything is a fable.)

Poetik: Im Märchen glaub ich am besten meine Gemütsstimmung ausdrücken zu können. (Alles ist ein Märchen.)

(*Das allgemeine Brouillon 1798–9*, *Gesammelte Werke*, No. 2281, vol. IV, p. 126.)

* * * * *

The fable is, as it were, the canon of poetry – everything poetic must be like a fable. The poet worships coincidence.

Das Märchen ist gleichsam der Kanon der Poesie – alles Poetische muss märchenhaft sein. Der Dichter betet den Zufall an.

(*Das allgemeine Brouillon 1798–9*, *Gesammelte Werke*, No. 2403, vol. IV, p. 165.)

* * * * *

A fable is really like a dream image without connections, an ensemble of wondrous things and happenings, e.g. a musical fantasy, the harmonious sequences of an aeolian harp – nature itself.

Ein Märchen ist eigentlich wie ein Traumbild ohne Zusammenhang, ein Ensemble wunderbarer Dinge und Begebenheiten, z.B. eine musikalische Fantasie, die harmonischen Folgen einer Aolsharfe – die Natur selbst.

(*Das allgemeine Brouillon 1798–9*, *Gesammelte Werke*, No. 2447, vol. IV, p. 172.)

*   *   *   *   *

A novel must be poetry through and through. For poetry is, like philosophy, a harmonious mood of our spirits, in which everything becomes more beautiful, each thing has its appropriate view, everything its fitting accompaniment and framework. In a truly poetic book everything seems so natural and yet so wondrous. One feels as though it could not be any other way, and it is as if one had been dozing in the world and were only now awakening to a true sense of the world. All remembrance and foreboding seems to spring from this source. Likewise, that present, where one is caught in illusion – single hours, in which one is, as it were, within all the objects one contemplates and experiences the infinite, incomprehensible, simultaneous feelings of a cohesive pluralism.

Ein Roman muss durch und durch Poesie sein. Die Poesie ist nämlich, wie die Philosophie, eine harmonische Stimmung unsers Gemüts, wo sich alles verschönert, wo jedes Ding seine gehörige Ansicht, alles seine passende Begleitung und Umgebung findet. Es scheint in einem echt poetischen Buche alles so natürlich und doch so wunderbar. Man glaubt, es könne nichts anders sein und als habe man nur bisher in der Welt geschlummert und gehe einem nun erst der rechte Sinn für die Welt auf. Alle Erinnerung und Ahndung scheint aus eben dieser Quelle zu sein. So auch diejenige Gegenwart, wo man in Illusion befangen ist – einzelne Stunden, wo man gleichzeitigen Empfindungen eines zusammenstimmenden Pluralis fühlt.

(*Fragmente aus den letzten Jahren 1799–1800*, *Gesammelte Werke*, No. 2638, vol. IV, p. 212.)

* * * * *

Truly romantic prose, highly varied, wondrous – strange turns, rapid jumps – wholly dramatic. Also for short essays.

Eigentliche romantische Prosa, höchst abwechselnd, wunderbar – sonderliche Wendungen; rasche Sprünge – durchaus dramatisch. Auch zu kleinen Aufsätzen.

(*Fragmente aus den letzten Jahren 1799–1800*, *Gesammelte Werke*, No. 2714, vol. IV, p. 229.)

* * * * *

Narratives, unconnected, yet full of associations, like dreams. Poems, simply fine-sounding and full of beautiful words, but also devoid of meaning and connection, at most isolated stanzas comprehensible; they must, like fragmented pieces, be made up of the most diverse things. At most true poetry can have an allegorical meaning in its totality and an indirect effect, like music etc.

Erzählungen ohne Zusammenhang, jedoch mit Assoziation, wie Träume. Gedichte, bloss wohlklingend und voll schöner Worte, aber auch ohne allen Sinn und Zusammenhang, höchstens einzelne Strophen verständlich; sie müssen wie lauter Bruchstücke aus den verschiedenartigsten Dingen sein. Höchstens kann wahre Poesie einen allegorischen Sinn im grossen haben und eine indirekte Wirkung wie Musik etc. tun.

(*Fragmente aus den letzten Jahren 1799–1800*,
Gesammelte Werke, No. 2899, vol. IV, p. 266.)

FRIEDRICH SCHLEGEL

Yesterday, when the argument was at its liveliest, you asked me for a definition of the novel; in such a way, as if you already knew, you would get no satisfactory answer. I do not consider this problem insoluble. A novel is a romantic book.* – You will dismiss this as a meaningless tautology. But I want first just to remind you that with a book one thinks already of a work, an independent whole. There is thus a very important distinction from drama, which is destined to be viewed; the novel, on the other hand, has since ancient times been intended for reading, and from this can be deduced nearly all the divergences in the manner of presentation in the two forms. Drama should be romantic, like all poetry, but a novel is romantic only with certain limitations, as an applied novel. The dramatic thread of the story does not by any means make it a whole, a work, unless it becomes so through the relationships of the entire composition to a higher unity than the literal one, which it often disregards, as it well may, through the nexus of ideas, the spiritual centre.

Apart from this, there is so little antithesis between drama and novel that drama, if it is interpreted and handled as thoroughly and historically as Shakespeare, for example, does, is the true foundation of the novel. You maintain, to be sure, that the novel is most closely related to the narrative, indeed to the epic genre. In response I remind you first, that a song can be just as romantic as a story. In fact, I cannot conceive of a novel

---

* There is a pun in the German that is untranslatable. The word 'Roman', the customary German term for 'novel', is derived, like 'romantisch', from *romance*.

other than as a mixture of narrative, song and other forms.

Sie verlangten gestern, da der Streit eben am lebhaftesten wurde, eine Definition, was ein Roman sei; mit einer Art, als wüssten Sie schon, Sie würden keine befriedigende Antwort bekommen. Ich halte dieses Problem eben nicht für unauflöslich. Ein Roman ist ein romantisches Buch. – Sie werden das für eine nichtssagende Tautologie ausgeben. Aber ich will Sie zuerst nur darauf aufmerksam machen, dass man sich bei einem Buche schon ein Werk, ein für sich bestehendes Ganze denkt. Alsdann liegt ein sehr wichtiger Gegensatz gegen das Schauspiel darin, welches bestimmt ist angeschaut zu werden: der Roman hingegen war es von den ältesten Zeiten für die Lektüre, und daraus lassen sich fast alle Verschiedenheiten in der Manier der Darstellung beider Formen herleiten. Das Schauspiel soll auch romantisch sein, wie alle Dichtkunst; aber ein Roman ists nur unter gewissen Einschränkungen, ein angewandter Roman. Der dramatische Zusammenhang der Geschichte macht den Roman im Gegenteil noch keineswegs zum Ganzen, zum Werk, wenn er es nicht durch die Beziehung der ganzen Komposition auf eine höhere Einheit, als jene Einheit des Buchstabens, über die er sich oft wegsetzt und wegsetzen darf, durch das Band der Ideen, durch einen geistigen Zentralpunkt wird.

Dies abgerechnet, findet sonst so wenig ein Gegensatz zwischen dem Drama und dem Roman statt, dass vielmehr das Drama so gründlich und historisch wie es Shakespeare z.B. nimmt und behandelt, die wahre Grundlage des Romans ist. Sie behaupteten zwar, der Roman habe am meisten Verwandtschaft mit der erzählenden ja mit der epischen Gattung. Dagegen erinnre ich nun erstlich, dass ein Lied ebenso gut romantisch sein kann als eine Geschichte. Ja ich kann mir einen Roman kaum anders denken, als gemischt aus Erzählung, Gesang und andern Formen.

(Gespräch über die Poesie, Kritische Ausgabe, vol. II, pp. 335–6.)

LYRIC POETRY

NOVALIS

It would be a subtle question to ask: whether the lyric poem were really a poem, superpoetry, or prose, infrapoetry? Just as the novel was regarded as prose, so the lyric was regarded as poetry – both wrongly. The highest, truest prose is the lyric poem.

Es wäre eine artige Frage, ob denn das lyrische Gedicht eigentlich Gedicht, Pluspoesie, oder Prosa, Minuspoesie wäre? Wie man den Roman für Prosa gehalten hat, so hat man das lyrische Gedicht für Poesie gehalten – beides mit Unrecht. Die höchste, eigentlichste Prosa ist das lyrische Gedicht.

(*Fragmente des Jahres 1798, Gesammelte Werke*, No. 827, vol. III, p. 27.)

WILLIAM WORDSWORTH

The reader will find that personifications of abstract ideas rarely occur in these volumes; and are utterly rejected, as an ordinary device to elevate the style, and raise it above prose. My purpose was to imitate, and, as far as possible, to adopt the very language of men; and assuredly such personifications do not make any natural or regular part of that language. They are, indeed, a figure of speech occasionally prompted by passion, and I have made use of them as such; but have endeavoured utterly to reject them as a mechanical device of style, or as a family language which Writers in metre seem to lay claim to by prescription.

(*Preface to 'Lyrical Ballads', Poetical Works*, vol. II, p. 390.)

*   *   *   *   *

By the foregoing quotation it has been shown that the language of Prose may yet be well adapted to Poetry; and it was previously asserted, that a large portion of the language of every good poem can in no respect differ from that of good Prose. We will go further. It may be safely affirmed, that there neither is, nor can be, any *essential* difference between the language of prose and metrical composition. We are fond of tracing the resemblance between Poetry and Painting, and, accordingly, we call them Sisters: but where shall we find bonds of connection sufficiently strict to typify the affinity betwixt metrical and prose composition? They both speak by and to the same organs; the bodies in which both of them are clothed may be said to be of the same substance, their affections are kindred, and almost identical, not necessarily differing even in degree; Poetry sheds no tears 'such as Angels weep' but natural and human tears; she can boast of no celestial ichor that distinguishes her vital juices from those of prose; the same human blood circulates through the veins of them both.

If it be affirmed that rhyme and metrical arrangement of themselves constitute a distinction which overturns what has just been said on the strict affinity of metrical language with that of prose, and paves the way for other artificial distinctions which the mind voluntarily admits, I answer that the language of such Poetry as is here recommended is, as far as is possible, a selection of the language really spoken by men; that this selection, wherever it is made with true taste and feeling, will of itself form a distinction far greater than would at first be imagined, and will entirely separate the composition from the vulgarity and meanness of ordinary life; and, if metre be superadded thereto, I believe that a dissimilitude will be produced altogether sufficient for the gratification of a rational mind.

(*Preface to 'Lyrical Ballads'*, *Poetical Works*, vol. II, p. 392.)

* * * * *

The poet thinks and feels in the spirit of human passions. How, then, can his language differ in any material degree from that of all other men who feel vividly and see clearly? It might be *proved* that it is impossible. But supposing that this were not the case, the Poet might then be allowed to use a peculiar language when expressing his feelings for his own gratification, or that of men like himself. But Poets do not write for Poets alone, but for men. Unless therefore we are advocates for that admiration which subsists upon ignorance, and that pleasure which arises from hearing what we do not understand, the Poet must descend from this supposed height; and, in order to excite rational sympathy, he must express himself as other men express themselves. To this it may be added, that while he is only selecting from the real language of men, or, which amounts to the same thing, composing accurately in the spirit of such selection, he is treading upon safe ground, and we know what we are to expect from him. Our feelings are the same with respect to metre; for, as it may be proper to remind the Reader, the distinction of metre is regular and uniform, and not, like that which is produced by what is usually called POETIC DICTION, arbitrary, and subject to infinite caprices upon which no calculation whatever can be made. In the one case, the Reader is utterly at the mercy of the Poet, respecting what imagery or diction he may choose to connect with the passion; whereas, in the other, the metre obeys certain laws, to which the Poet and Reader both willingly submit because they are certain, and because no interference is made by them with the passion, but such as the concurring testimony of ages has shown to heighten and improve the pleasure which co-exists with it.

(*Preface to 'Lyrical Ballads', Poetical Works*, vol. II, p. 398.)

*   *   *   *   *

The beauty of this stanza tempts me to conclude with a

principle which ought never to be lost sight of, and which has been my chief guide in all I have said, – namely, that in works of *imagination and sentiment*, for of these only have I been treating, in proportion as ideas and feelings are valuable, whether the composition be in prose or in verse, they require and exact one and the same language. Metre is but adventitious to composition, and the phraseology for which that passport is necessary, even where it may be graceful at all, will be little valued by the judicious.

(*Preface to 'Lyrical Ballads', Poetical Works*, vol. II, pp. 408–9.)

SAMUEL TAYLOR COLERIDGE

One point then alone remains, but that the most important; its examination having been, indeed, my chief inducement for the preceding inquisition. '*There neither is or can be any essential difference between the language of prose and metrical composition.*' Such is Mr Wordsworth's assertion. Now prose itself, at least in all argumentative and consecutive works, differs, and ought to differ, from the language of conversation; even as reading ought to differ from talking. Unless therefore the difference denied be that of the mere *words*, as materials common to all styles of writing, and not of the *style* itself in the universally admitted sense of the term, it might be naturally presumed that there must exist a still greater between the ordonnance of poetic composition and that of prose, than is expected to distinguish prose from ordinary conversation.

(*Biographia Literaria*, chapter 18, vol. II, pp. 45–6.)

*　　*　　*　　*　　*

I argue from the EFFECTS of metre. As far as metre acts in and for itself, it tends to increase the vivacity and susceptibility both of the general feelings and of the attention. This effect it produces by the continued excitement of surprize, and by the quick reciprocations of curiosity still gratified and still re-excited, which are too slight indeed to be at any one moment objects of distinct consciousness, yet become considerable in their aggregate influence. As a medicated atmosphere, or as wine during animated conversation; they act powerfully, though themselves unnoticed. Where, therefore, correspondent food and appropriate matter are not provided for the attention and feelings thus roused, there must needs be a disappointment felt; like that of leaping in the dark from the last step of a staircase, when we had prepared our muscles for a leap of three or four.

(*Biographia Literaria*, chapter 18, vol. II, p. 51.)

*   *   *   *   *

In poetry, in which every line, every phrase, may pass the ordeal of deliberation and deliberate choice, it is possible, and barely possible, to attain that ultimatum which I have ventured to propose as the infallible test of a blameless style; its *untranslatableness* in words of the same language without injury to the meaning. Be it observed, however, that I include in the *meaning* of a word not only its correspondent object, but likewise all the associations which it recalls. For language is framed to convey not the object alone, but likewise the character, mood and intentions of the person who is representing. In poetry it *is* practicable to preserve the diction uncorrupted by the affectations and misappropriations, which promiscuous authorship, and reading not promiscuous only because it is disproportionally most conversant with the compositions of the day, have rendered general.

(*Biographia Literaria*, chapter 22, vol. II, pp. 115–16.)

PERCY BYSSHE SHELLEY

A poem is the image of life expressed in its eternal truth. There is this difference between a story and a poem, that a story is a catalogue of detached facts, which have no other bond of connexion than time, place, circumstance, cause and effect; the other is the creation of actions according to the unchangeable forms of human nature, as existing in the mind of the creator, which is itself the image of all other minds. The one is partial, and applies only to a definite period of time, and a certain combination of events which can never again recur; the other is universal, and contains within itself the germ of a relation to whatever motives or actions have place in the possible varieties of human nature. Time, which destroys the beauty and the use of the story of particular facts, stript of the poetry which should invest them, augments that of Poetry, and for ever develops new and wonderful applications of the eternal truth which it contains. Hence epitomes have been called the moths of just history; they eat out the poetry of it. The story of particular facts is as a mirror which obscures and distorts that which should be beautiful: Poetry is a mirror which makes beautiful that which is distorted.

(*A Defence of Poetry, Complete Works*, vol. VII, p. 115.)

*   *   *   *   *

For there is a certain order or rhythm belonging to each of these classes of mimetic representation, from which the hearer and the spectator receive an intenser and purer pleasure than from any other: the sense of an approximation to this order has been called taste by modern writers. Every man in the infancy of art, observes an order which approximates more or less closely to that from which this highest delight results: but the diversity is not sufficiently marked, as that its gradations should be sensible, except in those instances where the predominance of this faculty of approximation to the beautiful (for so we may be permitted to name the relation between this highest pleasure and its cause) is very great. Those in whom it exists in excess are poets, in the most universal sense of the word; and the pleasure resulting from the manner in which they express the influence of society or nature upon their own minds, communicates itself to others, and gathers a sort of reduplication from that community. Their language is vitally metaphorical; that is, it marks the before unapprehended relations of things and perpetuates their apprehension, until the words which represent them, become, through time, signs for portions or classes of thoughts instead of pictures of integral thoughts; and then if no new poets should arise to create afresh the associations which have been thus disorganised, language will be dead to all the nobler purposes of human intercourse.

(*A Defence of Poetry, Complete Works*, vol. VII,
p. III.)

ALEXANDRE SOUMET

The times are gone when pleasant maxims and blithe precepts were enough for inspiration. The imagination of the moderns must fathom more deeply the mysteries of our own hearts, and what we demand above all of our writers is that they should have, if I can put it this way, the genius for emotions. Ancient poetry, simple and resplendent, is like hope; modern poetry, idealistic and grave, is the reflection of remembrance. Religion, the ardour of lofty enthusiasms, the contemplation of nature and of the divinity: these are nowadays the favourite subjects of poetic meditation.

Les temps ne sont plus où d'aimables maximes et de riants préceptes suffisaient à l'inspiration. L'imagination des modernes a besoin de pénétrer plus avant dans les mystères de notre propre cœur, et ce que nous demandons avant tout à nos écrivains, c'est de posséder, si je puis m'exprimer ainsi, le génie des émotions. La poésie antique, fraîche et brillante, ressemble à l'espérance; la poésie moderne, idéale et sérieuse, est l'image du souvenir. La religion, l'enthousiasme des dévouements sublimes, la contemplation de la nature et de la divinité, sont aujourd'hui les plus chers objets de la rêverie des muses.

> (Review of Hugo's *Nouvelles Odes* in *La Muse française*; *Idées et doctrines littéraires du XIXe siècle*, ed.
> F. Vial & L. Denise, p. 95.)

VICTOR HUGO

The poet must have only one model, nature; only one guide, truth. He must not write with what has already been written, but with his soul and his heart.

Le poète ne doit avoir qu'un modèle, la nature; qu'un guide, la vérité. Il ne doit pas écrire avec ce qui a été écrit, mais avec son âme et son cœur.

> (1826 Preface to *Odes et Ballades*, *Œuvres poétiques*, vol. 1, p. 283.)

*   *   *   *   *

Revolutions, those splendid catalysts of change, revolutions transform everything, except the human heart. The human heart is like the earth: you can sow, plant, cultivate whatever you please on its surface: it will all the same go on bringing forth its natural vegetation, its wild flowers and fruits; but axes and probes will never plumb its depths; just as it will always be the earth, so the human heart will always be the human heart; the foundation of art, as the earth is of nature.

Les révolutions, ces glorieux changements d'âge de l'humanité, les révolutions transforment tout, excepté le cœur humain. Le cœur humain est comme la terre, on peut semer, on peut planter, on peut bâtir tout ce qu'on veut à sa surface: il n'en continuera pas moins à produire ses verdures, ses fleurs, ses fruits naturels; mais jamais pioches ni sondes ne le troubleront à de certaines profondeurs; mais de même qu'elle sera toujours la terre, il sera toujours le cœur humain; la base de l'art, comme elle de la nature.

(Preface to *Les Feuilles d'automne*, *Œuvres poétiques*, vol. I, p. 713.)

EMILE DESCHAMPS

André Chénier broke this antiquated yoke. He has, with genius, recreated the unaffected manner, the virile expression of the great poet, Régnier; and by returning to the early periods of our poetry, he has given back to our verse freedom from the cesura and from *enjambement*, and that lively, youthful pace, that had disappeared almost without trace. That is the mode of versification used by the contemporary school, which has also adopted from our old poets that elegant richness of rhyme, often disregarded during the past century; for rhyme is the characteristic feature of our poetry; it must be an adornment so as not to seem like a fetter, and lines shoddily rhymed are like lines that almost scan. This kind of verse has the great advantage of having been much less used, and particularly of affording far greater possibilities and variety; poetic narration seems to us possible only in this style. The regular pauses and plodding forms of other lines are intolerable in a lengthy poem; admiration soon turns into weariness.

André Chénier a rompu ce joug usé. Il a reproduit avec génie la manière franche, l'expression mâle du grand poète Régnier; et remontant aux premiers âges de notre poésie, il a rendu à nos vers l'indépendance de la césure et de l'enjambement, et cette allure jeune et vive, dont ils n'avaient presque plus de traces. C'est le mode de versification que suit l'école actuelle, qui a repris aussi à nos anciens poètes cette richesse élégante de rimes, trop négligée dans le dernier siècle; car la rime est le trait caractéristique de notre poésie, il faut qu'elle soit une parure, pour n'avoir pas l'air d'une chaîne, et des vers rimés à peu près sont comme des vers qui auraient presque la mesure. Cette sorte de vers a le grand avantage d'avoir été beaucoup moins employée, et surtout d'offrir beaucoup plus de ressources et de variété; le récit poétique ne nous paraît même possible que de cette manière. Les repos réguliers et les formes carrées des autres vers sont insupportables dans un poème de longue haleine; l'admiration devient bientôt de la fatigue.

> (Preface to *Études françaises et étrangères*, *Idées et doctrines littéraires du XIXe siècle*, ed. F. Vial & L. Denise, p. 147.)

ALPHONSE DE LAMARTINE

Here are four books of poetry written just as they were felt, not arranged into any particular order or sequence: like nature, which has an order without showing it; genuine poems, devoid of pose, the testimony less of the poet than of the human being, the intimate, involuntary disclosure of his experiences day by day, pages from his inner life, prompted on occasion by sadness, at others by joy, by solitude and by the world, by despair or by hope, at times of sterility or inspiration, of fervour or aridity.

Voici quatre livres de poésies écrites comme elles ont été senties, sans liaison, sans suite, sans transition apparente: la nature en a, mais n'en montre pas; poésies réelles et non feintes, qui sentent moins le poète que l'homme même, révélation intime et involontaire de ses impressions de chaque jour, pages de sa vie intérieure inspirées tantôt par la tristesse, tantôt par la joie, par la solitude et par le monde, par le désespoir ou l'espérance, dans ses heures de sécheresse ou d'enthousiasme, de prière ou d'aridité.

('Avertissement' to the *Harmonies poétiques et religieuses*, *Œuvres complètes*, vol. II, p. 197.)

Part IV

CHRONOLOGICAL TABLE, BIOGRAPHICAL AND BIBLIOGRAPHICAL DATA

CHRONOLOGICAL TABLE

1797 Wackenroder, *Herzensergiessungen eines kunstliebenden Klosterbruders* (Outpourings from the Heart of an Art-loving Friar)

1798 Novalis, *Blütenstaub* (Pollen)

1798–1800 Novalis, *Fragmente*

1798–1800 Friedrich Schlegel, *Athenäum Fragmente*

1799 Blake, Letter to Dr Trusler

1800 Friedrich Schlegel, *Gespräch über die Poesie* (Dialogue on Poetry)

1800 Staël, *De la Littérature* (On Literature)

1800 Wordsworth, *Preface to 'Lyrical Ballads'*

1801 A. W. Schlegel, *Vorlesungen über schöne Kunst und Literatur* (Lectures on Fine Art and Literature)

1809 A. W. Schlegel, *Vorlesungen über dramatische Kunst und Literatur* (Lectures on Dramatic Art and Literature)

1810 Blake, *A Vision of the Last Judgement*

1810 Staël, *De L'Allemagne* (On Germany)

1814 Coleridge, *On the Principles of Genial Criticism*

1817 Coleridge, *Biographia Literaria*

1817 Keats, Letter to Benjamin Bailey

1818 Keats, Letter to John Taylor

1819 Hugo, 'Sur André Chénier'

1821 Shelley, *A Defence of Poetry*

1822 Hugo, *Odes*

1823 Stendhal, *Racine et Shakespeare*

1824–5 Duvergier de Hauranne & Ludovic Vitet in *Le Globe*
1825 Soumet, Review of Hugo's *Nouvelles Odes*
1826 Hugo, *Odes et Ballades*
1827 Hugo, *Préface de 'Cromwell'*
1827 Ballanche, *Orphée*
1828 Deschamps, *Études françaises et étrangères* (French and Foreign Studies)
1829 Vigny, 'Lettre à Lord xxx', *More de Venise*
1829 Hugo, *Hernani*
1830 Lamartine, *Harmonies poétiques et religieuses* (Poetic and Religious Harmonies)
1831 Hugo, *Les Feuilles d'automne* (Autumn Leaves)
1832 Vigny, *Stello*
1834 Lamartine, *Des Destinées de la Poésie*
1836 Musset, *Lettres de Dupuis et Contonet*

BIOGRAPHICAL AND BIBLIOGRAPHICAL DATA

BALLANCHE, PIERRE-SIMON, 1766–1847

Ballanche is the prime exponent of the mystical tendencies in French Romanticism. Together with Chateaubriand, whose friend he was, Ballanche was largely instrumental in the resurgence of religious mysticism in France. His early work, *Du sentiment considéré dans son rapport avec la littérature et les beaux-arts* (1801) (On Feeling considered in relation to Literature and the Fine Arts), is a potent exaltation of sensibility. Many of Ballanche's ideas are presented in two prose-poems that are re-interpretations of Greek myths: *Antigone* (1814) and *Orphée* (1827). The latter in particular celebrates the transcendental powers of the artist.

EDITION: *Œuvres complètes* (Geneva: Slatkine reprints, 1967).

BLAKE, WILLIAM, 1757–1827

Though regarded as 'an unfortunate lunatic' by some of his contemporaries, Blake has come to be recognised as one of the most original English poets. An engraver by profession, he combined his interests in poetry and in engraving by evolving a new method of printing, using etched copperplates. His *Songs of Innocence* (1789) and *Songs of Experience* (1794) are the first of his 'Illuminated Books', in which the texts are accompanied by illustrations that provide both decoration and explanation. He continued this fusion of verbal and pictorial expression in his major subsequent works: *The Marriage of Heaven and Hell* (1790–3), *Visions of the Daughters of Albion* (1793), *America, a Prophecy* (1793), *Europe, a Prophecy* (1794), *The Song of Los* (1795), *Milton* (1804–8), *A Vision of the Last Judgement* (1810), and *Jerusalem* (1804–20). These works show his growing absorption in mysticism, nurtured by his early intensive reading of the Bible, his fascination with Celtic mythology, and the impact of the philosopher-mystic, Swedenborg. Blake's inclination to mysticism underlies his emphatic affirmation of the primacy of the imagination, which is his main contribution to Romantic thought. It was another poet, Yeats, who coined the most fitting description of Blake by calling him 'a literal realist of the imagination'.

EDITION: *Complete Writings*, ed. Geoffrey Keynes (London & New York: Oxford University Press, 1966).

COLERIDGE, SAMUEL TAYLOR, 1772–1834

Coleridge achieved almost equal eminence as a poet and as an aesthetician. By temperament he was essentially imaginative and idealistic. In his early twenties, when he met Southey, he not only quickly came to share the latter's enthusiasm for the French Revolution; soon he was also making plans with Southey for a so-called Pantisocracy, a Utopian community, which was to be founded probably in the New World, but which never actually materialised. In 1795 Coleridge met Wordsworth and his sister, Dorothy, who came to live near him at Alfoxden; later he joined them in the Lake District. It was in order to finance a walking tour in Germany that Wordsworth and Coleridge wrote the *Lyrical Ballads* (1789). Coleridge's contribution to the collection was *The Rime of the Ancient Mariner*, in which he set out to make the supernatural seem natural. That is the source of the haunting effect of many of his finest poems, such as *Kubla Khan* and *Christabel* (both published 1816, but written earlier). It has been conjectured that some of his fantasies were stimulated by opium, to which he became addicted after about 1801. Partly as a result of his visit to Germany, Coleridge developed a serious interest in the German idealistic tradition in philosophy. The writings of Kant, Schelling and Fichte found a deep resonance in his own thinking, as can be seen from his *Biographia Literaria* (1817), his major aesthetic work. Coleridge does not seek to expound a systematic philosophy of art; rather, he examines in a pragmatic, and at times almost casual manner various aesthetic notions. Like Blake, though in a less flamboyant style, Coleridge insists on the supremacy of the creative imagination, which he distinguishes from merely reproductive fancy. His was, above all, an 'Inquiring Spirit', to use the title of a volume published posthumously in 1840. His thought proved seminal not only for the Romantics, but for subsequent generations too.

EDITION: *Biographia Literaria*, ed. J. Shawcross (London & New York: Oxford University Press, 1907; 9th reprint, 1973).

DESCHAMPS, EMILE, 1791–1871

Deschamps is one of the minor figures in French Romanticism; his role is more that of a publicist than of a creative writer, although he did publish both poems and short stories. He was one of the founders, in 1823, of the influential journal, *La Muse française*, and his translations and imitations (including versions of *Romeo and Juliet* in 1839 and of *Macbeth* in 1844) helped to stimulate interest in English, German and Spanish literature. His *Études françaises et étrangères* (1828) is known chiefly for its preface, which became an important manifesto of French

Romanticism through its advocacy of moderate innova
tion.

EDITION: *Idées et doctrines littéraires du XIXe siècle*, ed. Francisque Vial & Louis Denise (Paris: Delagrave, 1937).

DUVERGIER DE HAURANNE, PROSPER, 1798–1881

Duvergier de Hauranne was primarily a politician and historian,
active in the movement for electoral and parliamentary reform
in France. His two major works are devoted to this topic: *La
Réforme parlementaire et la réforme éléctorale* (1846), and the
Historie du gouvernement parlementaire en France de 1814 à 1848
(1857–73). Through the close association of politics and literature during the emergence of the Romantic movement in
France, Duvergier de Hauranne also became a vociferous cam-
paigner for literary reform.

EDITION: *Le Romantisme défini par 'Le Globe'*, ed. Pierre
Trahard (Paris: Presses françaises, 1925).

HUGO, VICTOR, 1802–85

Hugo was the most energetic innovator among the French
Romantics. Throughout the 1820s he was in the forefront of the
controversies surrounding the emergence of Romanticism in
France. His shifts of opinion in literary and political matters
gave the lead to many of his contemporaries, who rallied to his
Cénacle and its journal, *La Muse française*. Although he wrote
two famous novels, *Notre-Dame de Paris* (1830) and *Les Misé-
rables* (1862), his chief contribution to Romanticism lies in the
lyric and, above all, in drama. The actual play *Cromwell* is of
slight interest compared to its substantial preface, in which
Hugo expounded his view of history and gave his prescription
for the literature suited to the present, viz. Romantic drama.

The theories in this manifesto were put into practice in *Hernani* (1829), which provoked the notorious 'battle' between the supporters of Classicism and the Romantics in the theatre. In lyric poetry as in drama, Hugo was the champion of freedom. In drama this meant the freedom to mix at will verse and prose, tragedy and comedy, the beautiful and the grotesque. In the lyric, freedom implied a loosening of the traditional forms and the direct expression of the personal emotion pouring forth from the poet's heart. These are the tenets that underlie Hugo's early collections, notably *Odes et Ballades* (1826) and *Les Feuilles d'automne* (1831). Later in life, Hugo became increasingly involved in the tempestuous political vicissitudes of nineteenth-century France, and these concerns are reflected in his writing. He is considered one of France's greatest poets, and certainly a major formative influence and exponent of French Romanticism.

EDITIONS: *Hernani*, ed. Pierre Richard & Gérard Sablayrolles (Paris: Larousse, 1965).
Préface de 'Cromwell', ed. Annie Ubersfeld (Paris: Garnier-Flammarion, 1968).
Œuvres poétiques, ed. Pierre Albouy & Gaetan Picon (Paris: Gallimard, Édition Pléïade, vol. I, 1964).
Œuvres complètes (Paris: Société d'éditions littéraires et artistiques, 1927).

KEATS, JOHN, 1795–1821

Keats is perhaps the most poignant of the English Romantics. From his youth onwards, he was familiar with death. He came from a family beset by tuberculosis, and with his training as an apothecary and his knowledge of medicine, as he watched his brother Tom decline and die, he must surely have had some foreboding of his own early death. It is this that gives to his poetry its particular timbre, stemming from an intense pleasure in the beauties of life, blended with an ever present, though mellow melancholy. The great Odes: *To Autumn*, *To Melancholy*, *To a Nightingale*, *To a Grecian Urn* all reflect, in the most harmonious form and with an abundance of sensuous imagery, Keats' appreciation of the sublimity and transience of human life. He wrote no literary theory as such, but scattered in his lively letters are spontaneous expressions of his views on art.

EDITION: *The Letters of John Keats*, ed. Maurice Buxton Forman, 4th rev. ed. (London & New York: Oxford University Press, 1952).

LAMARTINE, ALPHONSE DE, 1790–1869

It is Lamartine's early volumes of poetry, the *Méditations poétiques* (1820), the *Nouvelles Méditations* (1823) and the *Harmonies poétiques et religieuses* (1830) that are of prime importance in the history of French literature. His first collection, the *Méditations poétiques*, not only caused a sensation on its publication, but also marks a decisive breakthrough of the Romantic manner. In a retrospective preface written in 1849, Lamartine claims that he replaced the conventional lyre of Parnassus with the strings of the human heart, stirred by true emotion. In such well-known poems as *Le Lac*, *L'Isolement*, and *L'Automne*, Lamartine poured out his grief at the death of his beloved and his feelings for nature in verses of melodious grace. The sincerity of his approach, the spontaneity and seeming artlessness of his style, as well as the suppleness of his verse, denoted real innovations in the French poetry of the period. His subsequent collections never equalled the impact of this first one, and though he continued to write throughout his life, his later years, following his election to parliament in 1833, were devoted mainly to statesmanship.

EDITION: *Œuvres complètes*, vol. II (Paris: chez l'auteur, rue de la Ville-l'Evêque, 43, 1860).

MUSSET, ALFRED DE, 1810–57

Musset has often been called the 'enfant terrible' of French Romanticism. His relationship to the movement is ambivalent. His poems, especially the quartet entitled *La Nuit de Mai*, *La Nuit de Décembre*, *La Nuit d'Août* and *La Nuit d'Octobre* (1835–7) have many of the features commonly associated with Romanticism: the direct expression of personal feeling, the apotheosis of the poet, the belief in the ennobling effect of suffering, the self-dramatisation, the intensity of tone, and the flexibility of the verse. In the partly autobiographical novel, *La Confession d'un enfant du siècle* (1836), Musset also shows a deep understanding of the Romantic temperament, but here already his detachment is evident in his ability to analyse the underlying problems. Of his dramas, *Lorenzaccio* (1834) treats a historico-political subject in a manner indebted to both Shakespeare and melodrama. His other plays, such as *Les Caprices de Marianne* (1833), *On ne badine pas avec l'amour* (1834), *Il ne faut jurer de rien* (1836), and *Il faut qu'une porte soit ouverte ou fermée* (1845), are witty comedies, though not without a potentially tragic undercurrent. Yet in spite of his affiliation to the Romantic group known as the *Cénacle*, and in spite of his own use of Romantic motifs and techniques, in the *Lettres de Dupuis et Cotonet* (1836) Musset wrote a mordant satire on the movement.

EDITION: *Œuvres complètes*, ed. Maurice Allemand, vol. III (Paris: Gallimard, Edition Pléiade, 1957).

NOVALIS (pseudonym of HARDENBERG, FRIEDRICH VON), 1772–1801

Novalis is the outstanding creative poet of the first generation of German Romantics. He came from a family steeped in the Pietistic tradition, and in spite of his scientific training as a mining engineer, his natural inclination was towards mysticism.

His *Hymnen an die Nacht* (1800) (Hymns to the Night), written on the death of his beloved, celebrate his visions at her grave in ecstatic rhythms. His two narratives, *Heinrich von Ofterdingen* (Henry of Ofterdingen) and *Die Lehrlinge zu Saïs* (The Disciples at Saïs) remained unfinished and were published posthumously in 1802. Both tell of a youth's search for the inner meaning of life in poetry and nature. Novalis recorded his views on art, the artist, and a great variety of other topics in a large number of aphorisms. Some of these were included in Friedrich Schlegel's journal, *Athenäum*, some were collected under the title *Blütenstaub* (1798) (Pollen), while others were not edited until long after his death. These so-called 'fragments', generally written in a loose, dithyrambic style with a minimum of punctuation, show an intensely original, agile and speculative mind working by intuition and suggestion.

EDITION: *Gesammelte Werke*, ed. Carl Seelig (Zurich: Bühl-Verlag; vol. II, 1945; vols. III & IV, 1946).

SCHLEGEL, AUGUST WILHELM VON, 1767–1845

August Wilhelm Schlegel was, with his younger brother, Friedrich Schlegel, the leading theoretician of German Romanticism. He was one of the founder members of the first German Romantic group in Berlin and later in Jena, and it was he who was instrumental in the spread of German Romantic aesthetics throughout Europe. Of a less innovative but more systematic turn of mind than his brother, he was well able to organise the insights of the German Romantics into a coherent order. As tutor to Mme de Staël's children, he travelled from 1804 onwards in France, Italy, Sweden and England, and at her home in Coppet he also made wide acquaintance with European thinkers and writers, to whom he transmitted the ideas of German Romanticism. These were publicly disseminated in his *Vorlesungen über schöne Kunst und Literatur* (Lectures on Fine

Art and Literature) held in Berlin in 1801, and in the even more influential grandiose survey of the history of drama in his *Vorlesungen über dramatische Kunst und Literatur* (Lectures on Dramatic Art and Literature) in Vienna in 1808. Outstanding among his translations, which included works by Calderón, Dante, Petrarch, and the *Bhagavadgita*, is the Shakespeare version, undertaken in collaboration with Ludwig Tieck, and still in use in Germany today. A. W. Schlegel was highly important not only for his clear distinction between the Classical and the Romantic, but also for the subsequent development of Symbolism and modern aesthetics through his recognition that symbols, pictures and signs were the major means of representing and communicating the poet's perception of beauty.

EDITION: *Kritische Schriften und Briefe*, ed. Edgar Lohner (Stuttgart: Kohlhammer; vol. II, *Die Kunstlehre*, 1963; vols. V & VI, 1966 & 1967).

SCHLEGEL, FRIEDRICH VON, 1771–1829

Together with his elder brother, August Wilhelm Schlegel, Friedrich Schlegel was one of the prime movers of German Romanticism. He founded the journal *Athenäum* (1798–1800), where he published his philosophical and literary aphorisms as well as his *Gespräch über die Poesie* (1800) (Dialogue on Poetry), which contains many seminal ideas for his later thought, particularly on mythology and on the narrative. His only novel, *Lucinde* (1799), infamous at the time of publication for its alleged advocacy of free love, is now seen as an early forerunner of the experimental novel. Friedrich Schlegel's chief importance lies in the scope and originality of his aesthetic theories. He extolled the work of art, the free expression of the creative imagination, as the summit of man's achievement. His lively and capacious mind ranged from Classical Antiquity to Oriental studies and the philosophy of history and religion. His thinking is often complex and at times opaque, not least on account of his preference for seemingly paradoxical formulations. Yet his ideas, in their very extremism, are not only basic to the Romantic conception of art, but also crucial to the evolution of modern aesthetics.

EDITION: *Kritische Ausgabe*, vol. II, *Charakteristiken und Kritiken* (1796–1801), ed. Hans Eichner (Munich-Padeborn-Vienna: Schöningh, 1967).

SHELLEY, PERCY BYSSHE, 1792–1822

Shelley was the most versatile of the English Romantics. His rebellious and impulsive nature led him into a tempestuous life of emotional involvements, travel, and personal misfortunes, ending with his death by drowning in Italy. His lasting fame rests on a series of brilliant lyric poems, mostly written in an extraordinary burst of his mature creative powers during the last four years of his life: *Ode to the West Wind, The Cloud, To A Skylark, A Dirge, To Night, Song, Stanzas Written in Dejection, near Naples*. They capture the fleeting mood of the moment – of elation, or more often of melancholy – in a dazzling succession of sensuous images. Shelley also wrote longer narrative poems, such as *Adonais* (1821), *Epipsychidion* (1821), and the *Triumph of Life* (1824), and lyrical dramas, including *Prometheus Unbound* (1820), and *The Cenci* (1821). Of his reflective prose, the most important is *A Defence of Poetry* (1821). Composed in reply to Thomas Love Peacock's *The Four Ages of Poetry*, which argued that poetry was in the last stages of its decline, Shelley's *Defence of Poetry* is an unequivocal rebuttal in the form of an eloquent assertion of the idealistic conception of poetry and the poet and of their function in life.

EDITION: *Complete Works*, ed. Roger Ingpen & Walter E. Peck, vol. VII (London: Benn, & New York: Scribner's, 1930).

SOUMET, ALEXANDRE, 1788–1845

A writer and critic, Soumet was, like many of the French Romantics, also involved in politics. Though first a supporter of Napoleon, he became a Royalist on the Bourbon Restoration, and held appointments as librarian in the palaces at St Cloud (1822) and Rambouillet (1824). He wrote a series of tragedies on Biblical, mythological and historical subjects in the 1820s, and in 1840 an epic poem, *La Divine Épopée*. He made his mark as a critic with *Les Scrupules littéraires de Mme. de Staël* (1814). His reviews and occasional articles in journals are forthright but moderate.

EDITION: *Idées et doctrines littéraires du XIXe siècle*, ed. Francisque Vial & Louis Denise (Paris: Delagrave, 1937).

STAËL, ANNE-LOUISE-GERMAINE DE, 1766–1817

One of the most colourful figures of her age, Madame de Staël, as she is generally known, derived her name from her Swedish husband, Baron de Staël-Holstein. She was the daughter of the Swiss financier, Jacques Necker, a minister of Louis XIV, and she grew up in Paris in the splendid salons of the pre-Revolutionary years. She soon became famous for her brilliant intellect, her independence, and her adventurous life. Her political liberalism and her irrepressible candour antagonised Napoleon, who banished her from France. After extensive travels in Germany, Russia, Italy and England, she settled at Coppet, near Geneva. Her 'court' there became a meeting-place for many leading European thinkers and writers and a forum for the discussion of ideas, both political and literary. Though she published two novels, *Delphine* (1803) and *Corinne* (1807), her lasting importance lies in her polemical critical works, *De la Littérature considérée dans ses rapports avec les institutions sociales*

(1800) (On Literature Considered in Relation to Social Institutions) and *De L'Allemagne* (1810) (On Germany). Written with great verve, both express notions that are perhaps idiosyncratic, but that are provocative and stimulating, above all through their championship of the so-called literature of the North as an alternative to the Classical tradition dominant in France.

EDITIONS: *De la Littérature*, ed. Paul van Tieghem (Geneva: Droz, & Paris: Minard, 1959).
De L'Allemagne, ed. Jean de Pange & Simone Balayé (Paris: Hachette, vol. II, 1958).

STENDHAL (pseudonym of BEYLE, HENRI), 1783–1843

Stendhal is known foremost as a novelist; *Le Rouge et le Noir* (1830) (The Red and the Black) and *La Chartreuse de Parme* (1839) (The Charterhouse of Parma) are undoubtedly among the greatest European novels. But he was also active first in the army during the Napoleonic reign, and later as French consul in various Italian cities. Between 1821 and 1830, at the height of the controversies surrounding the emergence of the Romantic movement in France, Stendhal lived in Paris and frequented the salons, where he became involved in the vehement political and literary debates. His *Racine et Shakespeare* (1823–5) is one of the earliest and most crucial manifestoes of French Romanticism. Its outspoken statement of the alternative modes in drama was a landmark in the emancipation of the French theatre from an antiquated system of restrictive rules.

EDITION: *Racine et Shakespeare* (Paris: Editions Pauvert, 1965).

VIGNY, ALFRED DE, 1797–1863

Vigny has, with some justification, been described as 'the intellectual' of the French Romantic movement. An aristocrat by birth, a Royalist by inclination, and an army officer by profession, Vigny maintained a certain distance, inner as well as outer, from his contemporaries. His two major collections of poetry, the *Poèmes antiques et modernes* (1826) and *Les Destinées* (1846), eschew both the outpouring of feeling and the metrical innovations practised by the Romantics. Instead, in such fine poems as *Moïse*, *La Colère de Samson*, *La Mort du Loup*, *Le Mont des Oliviers* and *L'Esprit Pur*, Vigny upholds stoicism and nobility of the mind in elegantly controlled verses. Through his marriage to an Englishwoman and his visits to England, he developed an interest in English literature. His play, *Chatterton* (1835), is a portrayal of the English poet as an example of the misunderstood genius. This is also the dominant theme of *Stello* (1832), in which Gilbert and André Chénier are aligned with Chatterton. Vigny's main contribution to French Romanticism lay in his translations and adaptations of Shakespeare: *Romeo and Juliet* in 1827, *Othello* in 1829, and *The Merchant of Venice* in 1830. Under the impact of Shakespeare, Vigny made forthright and astringent suggestions for the renewal of the French theatre.

EDITION: *Œuvres complètes*, ed. F. Baldensperger (Paris: Gallimard, Édition Pléïade, 1950).

VITET, LUDOVIC (LOUIS), 1802–73

Vitet began his career by writing for the journal *Le Globe*, and by authoring a dramatic trilogy under the title *La Ligue* (1826–9). After 1830, when he was appointed inspector of ancient monuments, his interests turned more towards history and politics. He published a *Histoire de Dieppe* (1833), was elected to parliament in 1834, and rose to become vice-president of the State Council.

EDITION: *Le Romantisme défini par 'Le Globe'*, ed. Pierre Trahard (Paris: Presses françaises, 1925).

WACKENRODER, WILHELM HEINRICH, 1773–98

Wackenroder was one of the earliest exponents of German Romanticism. While still a student, he visited Nuremberg and Dresden with his friend and subsequent collaborator, Ludwig Tieck. These old cities, together with the art of the Middle Ages, and particularly of Dürer, made a deep impression on him. He gave vent to his enthusiasms in the *Herzensergiessungen eines kunstliebenden Klosterbruders* (1797) (Outpourings from the Heart of an Art-loving Friar). This rather bizarre title encompasses a varied collection of pieces about the visual arts and music, written in a rhapsodic, lyrical style. Whatever their subject, the pieces are all characterised by a fervent worship of art as a sacred object and of the artist as a quasi-divine creator. These views were to become cardinal tenets of European Romanticism.

EDITION: *Herzensergiessungen eines kunstliebenden Klosterbruders*, ed. A. Gillies (Oxford: Blackwell, 1948).

WORDSWORTH, WILLIAM, 1770–1850

Wordsworth is associated primarily with the poetry of nature and of simple rural life, particularly that of the Lake District, where he spent many years. He was not, however, a recluse in an idyll. In 1790, on a walking tour in France and Italy, he experienced the French Revolution, which he first welcomed with high hopes for the future of mankind, but which was subsequently to cause him grievous disillusionment, as he records in his poetic autobiography, *The Prelude* (1805, published posthumously). He is best known for the *Lyrical Ballads* (1798), written in collaboration with Coleridge to finance their visit to Germany. While Coleridge was to make the supernatural seem natural, Wordsworth was to give poetic illumination to the commonplace. This he did in such poems as *Simon Lee, We are*

Seven, The Thorn, Goody Blake and Harry Gill, The Idiot Boy, Lines written in Early Spring, Expostulation and Reply, and *Tintern Abbey*. Although the *Lyrical Ballads* are now considered a turning-point in the history of English poetry, marking the return to a simpler, more direct mode, they were not well received on their first appearance. It was to correct misunderstanding of his intentions that Wordsworth prefaced the second edition of 1800 with 'Observations' explaining his view of poetry. This *Preface to 'Lyrical Ballads'* became one of the most important documents of European Romanticism. Wordsworth continued to write throughout the rest of his life, and was appointed Poet Laureate in 1843, but his later poems do not equal the earlier in imaginative power.

EDITION: *Poetical Works*, ed. E. de Selincourt, vol. II (Oxford: Clarendon Press, 1944).

INDEX OF AUTHORS